NSPCC

Policy Practice Research Series

Child Neglect

Practitioners' Perspectives

by Bill Stone

The author

Bill Stone is a social work practitioner based in one of NSPCC's child protection teams in the North of England. He qualified as a social worker in 1981 and, since then, has worked in a variety of settings in the statutory and voluntary sectors. Over the past five years he has been developing a particular interest in issues around child neglect as both a researcher and a practitioner.

NSPCC

The National Society for the Prevention of Cruelty to Children (NSPCC) is the UK's leading charity specialising in child protection and the prevention of cruelty to children.

The NSPCC exists to prevent children from suffering abuse and is working for a future for children free from cruelty.

First published 1998 by the NSPCC
42 Curtain Road
London
EC2A 3NH

Tel: 0171 825 2500
Fax: 0171 825 2525
Email: nspcc-research@mailbox.ulcc.ac.uk

Registered charity number 216401

Design by Red Stone
Photo posed by model
Photography Matt Harris

ISBN 0 902498 77 0

Foreword

The issue of child neglect touches on some of the most sensitive aspects of the relationship between the family and the state, and raises many questions about the rights of the state to intervene in childrearing. More than any other child protection topic, neglect has been subject to changing expectations of parents in different cultures and at different times.

Different patterns of parental employment have affected the time available for children and the possibility of parental presence in the home; economic prosperity and depression affect expected standards of clothing and material care; medical developments continuously change the health care regarded as essential for all children, whether concerned with immunisation or the avoidance of passive smoking; and consciousness of possible dangers from traffic, drugs or strangers change the attitudes of parents towards supervision of their children outside the family home. What was regarded as normal parental care two or three generations ago might now be seen in some ways as poor care or neglectful parenting and in others as over protection.

The research described in this report identifies some of the ways in which neglect means different things to different people, and the possibility for resulting confusion and lack of communication. The study examines a multi-agency group of practitioners' definitions and understanding of neglect, and uses these insights to explore social workers' experience of working with individual families whose children were on the Child Protection Register because they were suffering significant harm as a result of neglect. By examining the definitions used in different professional groups, the consensus and in some instances the disagreements over usage among members of the same professions, the importance of articulating and addressing these differences is emphasised. Unless we speak the same language, we cannot work together effectively for the protection of children and the support of their families. The report notes that, without a distinctive and consensual social work approach to neglect, the scope for thoughtful, evidence based practice is severely limited.

Most significantly, the report records the sadness and frustration which practitioners in all professions describe as their own response to working with longstanding problems of child neglect, and contrasts this with the 'guarded optimism' felt in direct work with individual families. Many of the families with children registered as suffering 'significant harm' from neglect faced fearsome problems of poverty, deprivation, poor housing, illness and family discord. Most parents in these families had themselves experienced poor care in their own childhoods. The challenge for all agencies working in this field is to support both families and practitioners in what can sometimes seem an overwhelming task of overcoming these burdens.

Jim Harding
Director and Chief Executive

Acknowledgements

The author would like to thank the many people who have made this research possible. Thanks are due, firstly, to NSPCC Northern Region for allowing the author the time and the space to undertake the work. Thanks are also due to Steven Shardlow and Pete Marsh at the Department of Sociological Studies at Sheffield University who gave much needed advice on refining the research proposal and timetabling the work. Colleagues within the author's team and elsewhere gave support and encouragement without which the research would probably have never been completed. All the participants in the research project need to be acknowledged and thanked because this is their work too.

Pat Cawson at NSPCC National Centre deserves thanks for helping to transform the report from a thesis into something rather more accessible and user friendly, as does Suzanne Kayne for her help with the word processing.

Finally, as always, my thanks goes to my wife Jacky and children Charlotte, Sam and Joshua who have endured a greater measure of neglect whilst I have been doing this research than either I, or they, would have wished.

Contents

Tables

Summary of research and findings

Child neglect: the context

■ Practice experience in social work and recent research findings on the child protection system have suggested that neglect has a low profile compared to other forms of child maltreatment. Some evidence suggests that social workers find it difficult to work with child neglect. Neglect also achieves much less public awareness than physical or sexual abuse.

■ There is a question mark over whether neglected children should be conceptualised as children in need rather than in child protection terms, and whether this might offer a more constructive support to the children and their families.

Previous research on child neglect

■ There is definitional confusion over neglect, with many competing approaches, none of which appear to have received general acceptance among practitioners.

■ Medical and psychological approaches share an underlying commitment to the methods and language of the physical sciences and are grounded in concepts of disease and pathology. Medical and socio-medical studies concentrate on parental deficits, particularly maternal deficits. Psychological and socio-psychological studies more often conceptualise neglect in terms of disordered parent–child relationships. Some recent studies have moved towards a focus on the interaction between people and the environment in which they live.

■ Sociological research evidence specifically addressing child neglect is scarce and diffuse. The studies of societal response to child maltreatment are particularly salient to neglect, which strongly impinges on cultural expectations about child rearing and the relationship between the family and the state.

■ Studies of the social construction of child maltreatment focus on its perception and definition. These studies challenge the pathologising of parents, families and of particular social class or ethnic groups. They suggest that pathologising strategies are used to place problems of child maltreatment in the hands of medical or social work experts. This downplays responsibilities of the state for a social problem with economic and political aspects.

■ Some research has focused more pragmatically on public and professional consensus over what constitutes neglect. This has tended to show relatively high consensus, regardless of profession, social class or ethnicity. Most of this work is American and there is little British material.

■ Research on the child protection system has attempted to develop instruments to measure neglect and to examine the operation of child protection services in response to neglect. Results vary considerably, some studies suggesting limited consensus and few differences between neglected children and victims of abuse, while others found marked differences.

■ The scarcity of British material on neglect is particularly marked. There is a lack of material developing a distinctively social work approach to understanding and defining neglect, and in consequence the scope for thoughtful, evidence based social work practice is severely limited.

Practitioners' definitions of neglect

■ A research design was developed to examine the way in which families become defined by professionals as neglect cases. In the first stage, a workshop was held for 33 practitioners from agencies making up the Area Child Protection Committee in a metropolitan borough. Participants included social workers, health visitors, teachers, police and probation officers. They completed individual exercises and took part in focus groups.

■ In individual exercises, they were asked to construct their personal definition of neglect and to rate a series of 30 case scenarios of possible neglect. In the focus groups they were asked to assess children's needs, to identify significant features of neglect cases, and to describe their own feelings about working with child neglect.

■ Results of the individual definition exercise identified consensus on physical and emotional neglect in which the primary focus was on the concepts of needs and care. Primary needs such as food, clothing, shelter and medical care, and emotional needs such as love, were prominent. Although protection from harm and safety were concerns, lack of supervision of children was not mentioned as a feature of neglect in any individual definitions.

■ The case scenarios used had been developed in a study in the USA by Craft and Staudt (1991) and were adapted for language to the British scene. Respondents rated on two dimensions, whether a situation was considered dangerous and whether the child was to be referred for a child protection enquiry.

■ Results showed higher consensus on which scenarios were dangerous than on which were safe, and large areas where there was little agreement either to refer or on dangerousness. All items on the supervision of children and leaving children alone led to marked division of opinion.

■ There was relatively little relationship between the assessment of dangerousness and the decision to refer, showing the way in which a child protection enquiry could be used because of anxiety about the situation rather than because it was seen as immediately dangerous.

■ There was little identification of the context of neglect in the individual exercises, but discussion of significant features of neglect cases included a perception that neglectful behaviour was associated with a cycle of inter-generational transmission. Neglecting families were seen as resistant to official agencies, and in the majority of groups significant features included poverty, deprivation, poor housing and unemployment.

■ Practitioners' descriptions of their own feelings about working with child neglect were overwhelmingly negative, with almost all identifying sadness, despair, helplessness, anger and frustration.

Common themes in practitioners' assessment of neglect

■ In the second stage of the research, 20 individual cases of young children recently placed on the child protection register on the grounds of neglect were selected. The key social workers were interviewed with a schedule based on issues from the group exercises.

■ Key workers showed a high level of agreement with workshop participants on the significant features of neglect, and from a list of 35 features, identified more than 15 as present in 15 of the 20 cases. Three cases had more than 25 of the features.

■ In contrast to workshop participants, key workers were guardedly optimistic about the outcome for the families that they were working with. Their level of optimism was related to the age of the child, with early intervention leading to greater optimism.

■ Key workers' assessments supported the inter-generational transmission concept, and in 18 out of the 20 families, parents/carers were regarded as having been poorly parented themselves. Substance abuse, mental illness, learning disability, and domestic violence were also identified as significant features in a high proportion of the families.

■ As in the individual and focus group exercises, lack of supervision was not seen as a particular issue by individual key workers. Economic deprivation was a major feature in the families, with 18 considered to have financial problems.

Child neglect - a time for reappraisal

■ Results illustrated the complexity of child neglect, and the multiple difficulties which typified neglect cases. There appeared to be no one particular factor, which taken alone, could be used to define neglect. On some issues there is very limited professional consensus. A surprising finding was the apparent unimportance of lack of supervision to practitioners.

■ Results showed that practitioners considered emotional and relational factors to be essential to a definition of neglect and that poor material care alone would not be considered sufficient. Relationship issues and family dysfunction are central to practitioners' understandings of how children become neglected.

■ It was evident, however, that social factors connected with poverty and deprivation were important. Neglected children suffered from poverty both in their material and their emotional environments.

■ This is a small study in one local area, giving a snapshot of a situation at a particular moment in time. However, the variety of methods used has enabled the concepts to be examined from several different angles, and identified a number of significant themes. It indicates the importance of addressing questions of professional consensus over neglect, and of articulating and examining differences in definition and judgement, if children are to be given consistent support and adequate protection.

NSPCC 1998
Bill Stone

1 Child neglect: the context

Introduction

Child protection social work is acknowledged as being a difficult and challenging occupation. It is a high risk job which demands of its practitioners that they make judgements and take decisions which have far reaching implications for the lives of service users. It is also a high profile profession which is regularly exposed to hostile public scrutiny in response to child abuse scandals and tragedies (Cooper, 1995). Social workers deal with the stuff of everyday life; everybody has an opinion about how children should be brought up. Ideas about family relationships, mother love and child rearing are part of the common currency of life.

In this context child protection workers are routinely exposed to two contradictory criticisms. On the one hand they are accused of being overprotective of children and over-intrusive into family life or, in words frequently seen screaming from tabloid headlines, of 'tearing families apart'. On the other hand child protection social workers are criticised for being naive, ineffectual and indecisive, unwilling to intervene and rescue children from dysfunctional and dangerous families. The question of the threshold of intervention becomes absolutely crucial. At what point are child protection agencies justified in intervening to protect children?

The Children Act (1989) answers this question in terms of the concept of 'significant harm' and it seems possible that this form of words will gradually replace the powerful and emotive expression 'child abuse'. Yet significant harm is no more self evident than is child abuse, it needs to be both defined and evidenced in a systematic and rigorous way. This is not simply to satisfy the courts but also in the interests of the children who become subject to the child protection process. It is this question of significant harm in relation to child neglect which forms the backdrop to this research.

The child protection worker operating in the controversial and conflictual climate described above, needs to feel that the work that she/he does can be justified, and that it has some substance and value. In order to face the painful dilemmas which are an inescapable feature of the work, she/he needs to know that child protection can be defended intellectually, and that it has a rational basis of agreed knowledge based on valid research. From the point of view of the social work profession in the UK, research is at a premium (Lindsey and Kirk, 1992). The development of a research based culture is one of the major challenges facing social work. In terms of its professional credibility social work desperately needs more research, not just at the level of social work theory, but also evaluative research which takes a critical look at current practice.

Child neglect exists in the overlap between the personal and the political and, as such, it raises broader social questions about the place of children and child care in society. It raises questions about gender roles, child rearing cultures and the damaging effects on children of poverty and deprivation. These social questions are inextricably linked to the narrower concerns of personal and family relationships.

Policy responses to child neglect as a social problem are determined by our conceptualisations of what it is (Baldwin and Spencer, 1993). It is not yet clear whether there is a public, or even a professional, consensus about what constitutes child neglect and so policy responses are correspondingly ambiguous.

Research into the identification and assessment of children who are at risk of significant harm through neglect could also make a contribution towards the development of better child protection services. Training, practice guidance and Area Child Protection Committee (ACPC) policies and procedures are the most immediately obvious areas which could benefit. In the longer term it must be hoped that neglected children will eventually get a better deal. The subject of child neglect demands a greater degree of professional attention and application; in relation to other forms of child maltreatment it has been neglected for far too long (Tomison, 1995).

Problems in practice and theory

The research began with a practice problem arising from the writer's experience as a child protection social worker with the National Society for the Prevention of Cruelty to Children (NSPCC). How do social workers identify and work with families in which children are being neglected? Neglect cases appeared to be accorded low priority in the child protection system. This was evidenced by the tendency of these cases to be dropped before case conference, the smaller number of registrations in this category and the lack of services for neglected children and their families. In this the UK differs markedly from the USA, where neglect forms half of all registered cases (McCurdy and Daro 1993).

Some evidence suggested that social workers seemed to find it very difficult to engage in planned, systematic interventions in neglect cases. Moore suggests that the experience of working with neglectful and chaotic families indicated that the pervasive sense of power-lessness and apathy present in many neglecting families was contagious and had a disabling effect on the worker, making focused intervention difficult (Moore, 1989).

Neglect also had a low profile in the public awareness of child welfare issues. Whereas physical abuse and sexual abuse were frequently reported and commented upon the media displayed relatively little interest in neglect, except in a few dramatic exceptional cases such as the 'home alone' cases which hit the headlines in the winter of 1994, and the major enquiry following the death of 'Paul' (Bridge Child Care Consultancy Service, 1995). This might be due to the fact that neglect is a long term developmental issue rather than a short term crisis. It also might be related to the fact that in neglect cases it is not always easy to know who to blame.

Neglect appeared to be poorly understood in terms of theory. This was reflected in the shortage of literature specifically about child neglect, the small number of research studies focusing specifically upon neglect and the absence of specialised professional training for practitioners in this area.

The first, and in some ways the most fundamental of the theoretical issues is that of definition. There are many different definitions of child neglect and little consistency between them. Definitions have been framed for differing reasons and reflect different priorities. For example there are medical, legal, social work, educational and research definitions (Rose and Meezan, 1993).

A second issue is that of the link between child abuse and neglect. How does neglect fit into the broad spectrum of child maltreatment and what relationship does it have to other forms of abuse? The writer's practice experience was that neglect is frequently present in families where there are also concerns about physical or sexual abuse. Equally, there was a blurred boundary between emotional abuse and neglect. What is distinctive about neglecting families as opposed to abusing families, or is neglect to be seen simply as a form of abuse?

Neglect has a number of distinctive features which sets it apart from other forms of child abuse. Unlike physical and sexual abuse, neglect is not necessarily intentional or deliberate.

Indeed considerations of intentionality may confuse the issue. Whereas abuse can be described as an act of commission, positive maltreatment or an 'act of desperation', neglect can more helpfully be seen as an act of omission, negative maltreatment or 'an act of despair' (Polansky et al, 1981). The distinction may be important in child protection in so far as responses to child abuse tend to be punitive and adversarial. It has sometimes been suggested that neglected children should be conceptualised as children in need rather than as victims of maltreatment, enabling societal responses to the problem of neglected children to be very different (Department of Health 1995)

Another critical difference is that neglect does not commonly manifest itself in particular incidents. The time scale is different and with neglect the characteristic sense of urgency and danger may be absent. Neglect is a chronic problem rather than an acute crisis. It is the cumulative effect of neglect which is most damaging and neglecting families therefore require a response other than crisis intervention. The writer's practice experience suggested that social workers tend to ignore neglect cases until there is a specific incident of physical or sexual abuse. Because the child protection system is geared to investigating incidents, neglect may be overlooked. Similarly, because the orientation of professionals in the field is child protection rather than child welfare, neglect fits uneasily into the perennial preoccupation with child safety and child rescue.

Additionally, there is the question of how the causation of neglect should be understood. Three quite different approaches appeared to be current within child protection (Hutchinson, 1990). One saw neglect as being primarily a result of parental deficits and appeared to be most popular amongst those with a broadly psychological approach to the problem. Another emphasised the importance of social factors like poverty and deprivation. This seemed to be favoured by social workers with a community work orientation. There were those who attempted a synthesis emphasising the multi-factorial nature of neglect, and this seemed to be the approach which academics found most satisfying. Each of these constructions of neglect suggest different styles of intervention, so it seemed important to attempt to find out how practitioners conceptualise neglect in their ongoing work with neglecting families.

The research objectives

The study concentrates on the identification and assessment of families in which there are concerns relating to neglect, which is constructed in terms of child protection rather than in broader terms such as the low status of children and their carers. To become a child protection issue, neglect has to be severe enough for there to be a significant risk of harm to the children concerned, and the concentration therefore is on the more severely neglectful end of the child care continuum.

Child neglect is a very large field of study to which contributions have been made by a number of different disciplines. The scope of this research has been necessarily limited to give manageable areas of enquiry. The research is not able to examine the long term damaging effects of neglect in the lives of developing children, nor look at the most effective ways of preventing neglect or intervening therapeutically in such cases.

Finally, this is practitioner research in the sense that it is a view from within rather than observations from afar. The research describes what happens in practice rather than what ought to happen, although description of what currently happens may well lead to prescriptions for change. The empirical approach attempts to avoid the danger of imposing a one-dimensional view of neglect on a complex, multi-dimensional problem whilst doing justice to the genuine differences of opinion as to what constitutes child neglect which may obtain within the child protection community.

The primary question, 'What is meant, in an operational sense, by child neglect?' can be broken down into more precise questions:

1. How do child protection professionals distinguish between families in which children are being neglected from families in which children are not being neglected?

2. What working definitions do child protection professionals use to help them identify neglectful families?

3. What are the most significant defining features of families in which child neglect occurs and how do practitioners assess and evaluate these defining features?

The review of the literature given in the next chapter illustrates the multitude of approaches to defining and studying neglect from different perspectives. For this study it was necessary to reach an initial working definition of neglect as a starting point for examining practitioners' perspectives.

One definition which is relevant to the present study is that put forward by the Home Office, 'Working Together under the Children Act 1989' (Home Office et al, 1991). This is used by Area Child Protection Committees for purposes of registration and is a relatively strict and narrow one:

"Neglect: The persistent or severe neglect of a child, or the failure to protect a child from exposure to any kind of danger, including cold or starvation, or extreme failure to carry out important aspects of care, resulting in the significant impairment of the child's health or development, including non-organic failure to thrive." (p48)

A broader definition which has the merit of being simple to understand as well as being child focused is the one proposed by Dubowitz et al (1993, p12). They argue for a single, broad definition of neglect based on the concept that 'neglect occurs when the basic needs of children are not met, regardless of cause'. This is a helpful way of conceptualising the essence of neglect although, for child protection purposes, this definition would need to be tightened up and reformulated in terms of significant harm.

It was decided that Dubowitz et al's concept of unmet need was the most useful starting point for the present study because one of the main purposes of the research is to explore the question of definition. An underlying assumption is that there is not an agreed and precisely articulated operational definition of neglect which practitioners 'apply' to the various cases they deal with. Instead, the research pre-supposes that, whilst there is broad agreement on the general parameters around neglect, there is considerable scope for practitioners in the field to form their own judgements about how serious the neglect is in a particular case and what intervention is required. Thus practitioners develop, within the inter-agency child protection framework, their own operational definitions of neglect. It is hoped that looking at the factors which practitioners consider are most significant in this process will throw some light on the assessment of neglect. The breadth of Dubowitz et al's concept allows scope for the exploration of practitioners' meaning in their definitions of neglect.

2 Previous research on child neglect

Introduction

The review of the literature is in two sections. The first relates to conceptualisations of neglect, divided into medical / psychological and sociological approaches. The second section concerns responses to neglect, separated into legal / policy formulations and research into child protection practice. There appears to have been relatively little research focused specifically on neglect, compared to that available on other forms of maltreatment, particularly in the UK. Our understanding of neglect is heavily dependent on American literature, and the limitations of this for the British context must be taken into account (see Department of Health, 1995, pp94–96 for a discussion on the relevance of North American research on child protection). When appropriate this review includes

Figure 1 Child Neglect: a map of the literature

Theorising about neglect: theory

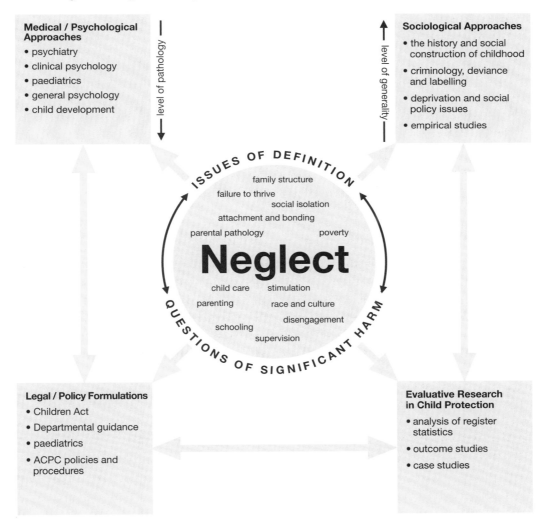

Medical / Psychological Approaches
- psychiatry
- clinical psychology
- paediatrics
- general psychology
- child development

level of pathology

Sociological Approaches
- the history and social construction of childhood
- criminology, deviance and labelling
- deprivation and social policy issues
- empirical studies

level of generality

ISSUES OF DEFINITION

family structure
failure to thrive
social isolation
attachment and bonding
parental pathology   poverty

Neglect

child care   stimulation
parenting   race and culture
                disengagement
schooling
supervision

QUESTIONS OF SIGNIFICANT HARM

Legal / Policy Formulations
- Children Act
- Departmental guidance
- paediatrics
- ACPC policies and procedures

Evaluative Research in Child Protection
- analysis of register statistics
- outcome studies
- case studies

Responding to neglect: practice

material from general studies of child maltreatment and from studies which include neglect as a sub category of abuse, where the findings as a whole have particular importance for the development of thinking about neglect. Figure 1 illustrates the sources of literature identified in this survey.

Definitional issues - child neglect, abuse and maltreatment

Definitional problems abound in child protection research and lead to all sorts of philosophical and methodological difficulties (Sassower and Grodin, 1990). Besharov (1981) argues the case for making definitional issues an explicit methodological concern in order to produce better research. Dingwall (1989) describes the amount of scientifically validated research on child abuse and neglect as 'vanishingly small'.

Cann (1989) also notes with concern the great potential for ambiguity in definitions of child abuse and neglect and advocates operational definitions, to include such factors as: type of abuse, severity, effect and duration. After reviewing different approaches to child maltreatment and pointing out that different definitions are devised for different purposes, Hutchinson advocates the use of a narrow definition in child protection with an explicit threshold for intervention (Hutchinson, 1990). Similar ground is covered with respect to child neglect by Rose and Meezan (1993). Dubowitz et al (1993) adopt an ecological perspective in their work on a conceptual definition of child neglect. Their definition helpfully focuses on the basic needs of children that are not met, rather than the intentions or behaviour of parents. They further suggest that responsibility for meeting these needs is shared between parents and the wider community.

Calam and Franchi (1987) developed a definition based on children's rights, rather than needs. They carried out a longitudinal study of abused children referred to an NSPCC Family Centre, adopting an observational approach. They concluded that children have a number of basic rights, the denial of which constitutes abuse or neglect, including the rights to be fed, clean, safe and valued. Their concepts however were developed from Kellmer Pringle's earlier formulation of the needs of children (Kellmer Pringle, 1975).

Hegar and Yungman (1989) attempt a causal typology of neglect, identifying three major categories: physical neglect, developmental neglect and emotional neglect. In an overview of neglect theorising Tzeng, Jackson and Karlson (1991) conclude, rather pessimistically, that there are:

"no theories or models of neglect per se that are currently being used by the service community." (p190)

This lack of consensus at the theoretical level leads to confusion around definition and to inconsistency and the rule of thumb at the operational level. Glachan (1991) reminds readers that a number of fundamental problems about child abuse and neglect have yet to be resolved. Firstly, there is the issue of exactly what behaviours should be regarded as abusive or neglectful and, secondly, whether the responsibility for abuse and neglect is best understood at an individual, family, social, cultural, or even wider economic and political level.

Approaches to neglect

In child protection some of the most interesting and significant debates are between different disciplines. The orientations of the various disciplines have a significant bearing on their conceptualisations of neglect (see Figure 1). Even within a single discipline, definitions of neglect are various, and many studies do not make their definitions explicit. Others use administrative categories such as inclusion on child protection registers as a definitional criterion. The following discussion of the literature reviews the findings in the context of the original authors' definitions and categories.

Medical and psychological research

Medical and psychological approaches have been grouped together because they tend to share a particular research methodology. They share a commitment to the physical as opposed to the social sciences and use the common language of the experimental method. They place a high value on quantitative data and the use of statistical techniques. In the background to their theorisations are more or less explicit concepts of disease and pathology.

These commonalities mask wide variations in the scope of the research and in the conceptualisations of neglect that they utilise. One way of differentiating between these approaches is to rank them according to degree of pathology. In broad terms psychiatry and clinical psychology concentrate on the negative end of the child care continuum, whilst child development is concerned with the optimal conditions for the normal growth and development of healthy children. Paediatrics and general medicine stand somewhere between these two extremes in the mainstream of medical practice.

Medical and socio-medical studies

In the context of psychiatry the work of Polansky and his associates is typical of that produced by researchers with a medical/psychological orientation. Polansky himself has a background in psychiatry and this is evident both in his theoretical orientation and his use of language which is very clinical and somewhat judgmental in tone. For example, whilst the terms 'infantilism' and 'impulse-ridden' may have a technical meaning to psychiatric practitioners, to the general reader they have strongly pejorative overtones.

Polansky's book 'Damaged Parents: An Anatomy of Neglect' (Polansky et al 1981) has the status of a classic text. Its title betrays the authors' underlying attitude to child neglect which locates the problem in psychological and developmental deficits within the parents which restrict their ability to care adequately for children. The book is based on two studies of low income families, the first in the rural southern Appalachians and the second in inner-city Philadelphia. In his attempt to discover what other factors, apart from low income, affect the level of parental care, Polansky concentrated on the mothers. His hypothesis was that neglectful mothers are likely to be 'character disordered' in some way. He concludes:

"the major findings of the Appalachian study were substantially supported in the Philadelphia replication. The mother's maturity or degree of infantilism was again underscored, as was its expression in the forms of apathy - futility or impulsivity."

In some of Polansky's later work the focus shifts from the individual pathology of the mother towards questions of family structure, social isolation and support networks. For example Polansky (1985) found that neglectful mothers reported less support from informal networks and described their neighbourhoods as less friendly and helpful than the control group (see also Hartley, 1989 and Nelson, Saunders and Landsman, 1993). In an article entitled 'Family Radicals' (Polansky, Gaudin and Kilpatrick 1992c) the chemical analogy of the radical is used to describe the intense volatility and changeability of neglectful families over time. Rather than being 'families' in any conventional sense of the word, they are portrayed as family fragments in changing constellations within which the mother-child bond is paramount.

In Britain, the Royal College of Psychiatrists' study 'Families without Hope', discovered that the mortality rate among neglectful families was almost double that among families where there was the same degree of poverty but no neglect (66 per thousand in neglectful families in contrast to 39 per thousand in the control group). The neglected children were more stunted, scored less well in IQ tests and had 30% more psychiatric disturbances

(Tonge, James and Hillam, 1975). The findings of this study need to be interpreted with some caution, so far as their implications for child protection are concerned, because the explicit focus of the study is on 'problem families' rather than neglectful families as such.

In a study of fatal child neglect Margolin (1990) found that fatalities appear to result from neglect at approximately the same frequency as from physical abuse, the most common scenario being that of the absence of the caregiver at the critical moment. Trube-Becker (1976) also looked at the deaths of children following negligence and concluded that the major cause was 'the incapacity and ignorance of mostly too young mothers'.

One field of study which is well represented, particularly by research with a medical orientation, is failure to thrive. This topic has a discrete literature of its own which overlaps with the literature on child neglect, but in a confusing and sometimes contradictory way. Children who fail to thrive are young children (failure to thrive is generally diagnosed only in infants and pre-school children) who fail to grow and develop physically, emotionally and intellectually in line with expectations. Failure to thrive tends to be defined operationally by health visitors as children whose weight is on or below the third centile, although it should be stressed that what is most significant is a downward deviation from the expected growth curve, especially when the child's growth is at the bottom of the normal range. Screening is therefore a vital issue and one which has important practical implications, (Batchelor, 1990; Wright, 1992).

'Working Together' (Home Office et al 1991) includes failure to thrive within its definition of neglect. Skuse (1992) however argues that: 'the importance of non-organic failure to thrive as a manifestation of abusive and neglectful child rearing practice has probably been overstated' (p108). He argues for a distinction to be made between failure to thrive which is now regarded primarily as a simple matter of under-nutrition, and 'psycho-social dwarfism' which he believes should be managed as a child protection problem. Moreover he asserts that there is no evidence from research in the UK that failure to thrive is especially common in deprived inner-city areas.

In a recent lecture on research into failure to thrive, Wright argued strongly that failure to thrive should not ordinarily be viewed as a child protection problem at all (Wright, 1996). The Parkin study monitored the entire child population of a particular area of Newcastle and identified those who were not thriving using 'the Thrive Index' a computer calculation based on velocity of weight gain. It was found that approximately 5% of the total child population was failing to thrive by this measure. These children, on closer examination, were very similar, socially and medically, to the children who were growing in the expected way. Wright concluded that whereas failure to thrive should not be assumed to be due to neglect, poverty or disease, it may be assumed to be due to undernutrition.

There seems to be an emerging consensus within the professional community that failure to thrive is primarily about nutrition even though the precise mechanisms which mediate this growth failure may not yet be fully understood. In paediatric practice therefore, whereas non-organic failure to thrive used to be a negative diagnosis (a diagnosis of last resort after the search for organic causes had proved elusive), it now tends to be a positive diagnosis which is primarily to do with nutrition and feeding difficulties (Berkowitz, Logan and Sklaren, 1985; Daws, 1994). In terms of management this means that interventions will be concentrated on issues around feeding - which may, incidentally, have significant emotional and relational aspects. Feeding an infant is an extremely highly charged process from an emotional point of view and the interactions between a parent and infant, at these critical times, have significant developmental implications (Hanks et al, 1988; Iwaniec, Herbert and Mcneish, 1985b; Iwaniec, 1995).

It is within mainstream paediatric medicine that some of the most persuasive advocates of the significance of neglect as a damaging experience for children may be found. The respect with which the general public accords paediatricians also gives them a platform from which they can argue the case for neglected children. Two such advocates, Hobbs and Wynne state:

"it is important to keep in mind that the greatest loss of human potential in childhood arises from neglect" (Hobbs, Hanks and Wynne, 1993, p10)

In association with Hanks, a psychologist, these two paediatricians have recently produced a 'Clinician's Handbook' (Hobbs, Hanks and Wynne, 1993) which has a comprehensive chapter on neglect. Most standard texts on child abuse and neglect have major contributions by medical practitioners and it is usually these, rather than social workers, lawyers or academics, who are invited to write the chapter on child neglect. In the USA, a prominent paediatrician, Dr Ray Helfer, has done a great deal to publicise the problem of child neglect (Helfer, 1990).

Psychological and socio-psychological studies

A number of studies with a base in psychology have approached the subject of child neglect in terms of disordered parent-child relationships. Fraiberg, Adelson and Shapiro (1975) adopted a psycho-analytic approach hypothesising that the mother's childhood experience affects her ability to parent (see also Brayden et al 1992). Covitz (1986) is a psychotherapist who looks at inability to meet children's emotional needs in terms of the 'family curse'. He argues that the effects of family disturbances are passed down through the generations but that their roots are to be found in childhood experiences. Other studies have made connections between the parent's (usually mother's) state of mental health and the quality of child care as, for example, does Polansky (1985).

Christensen et al (1994) looked at the connection between maternal self-esteem and parent-child interactions and found that low maternal self-esteem appears to be a risk factor for neglect. Seligman's classic theory of 'learned helplessness' (Seligman, 1972), which originated out of experimental work with dogs, suggests fruitful lines of enquiry as to the origin of neglectful behaviour in apathetic and listless parents. No studies have come to light which explicitly apply this theory to parenting behaviour, but there are treatment approaches which major on 'empowerment' as a means of challenging the perceived helplessness of neglecting parents.

Allocating causes exclusively or primarily to disordered relationships, however, has been challenged, both in studies of neglect and in broader studies of child maltreatment. In 1977 Bronfenbrenner published a significant article arguing for a different approach to the human sciences which is broader in its scope and which looks at the interactions between the human organism and the changing environments in which it lives (Bronfenbrenner, 1977). A number of social psychologists have developed this ecological approach and applied it to the field of child development and child protection.

Belsky (1993) in a wide ranging review of the literature on the causes of child maltreatment concludes:

"child maltreatment is now widely recognised to be multiply determined by a variety of factors operating through transactional processes at various levels of analysis in the broad ecology of parent-child relations" (p413)

Belsky emphasises that there is no single pathway to child maltreatment and that therefore the search for specific antecedents may be fruitless. Similar conclusions are reached by Ammerman (1990). Ammerman employs a behavioural perspective in the search for antecedents of child maltreatment, advocating the use of an ecological model which integrates causative variables at different levels.

In an attempt to understand the differences and commonalities of the various categories of child maltreatment a number of comparative studies have been undertaken. Milner and Robertson (1990) compared physical child abusers, intrafamilial child sex abusers and child neglecters. They found that all reported higher levels of personal distress than would be usual but that neglecters and physical abusers expressed more problems with their children. Dubowitz et al (1989) hypothesised that there was a considerable overlap in the aetiology of physical abuse and failure to thrive and found, after comparing the two groups, that they were indeed 'remarkably similar'. Jones and McCurdy (1992) looked at the links between types of maltreatment and the demographic characteristics of children. Out of the four categories of maltreatment (physical, sexual, neglect and emotional) they found that neglect was the most predictable and distinctive, largely because it was strongly associated with poverty. Clausen and Crittenden (1991) established strong associations between physical and psychological maltreatment and argued that more attention needs to be paid in child protection to psychological factors, (see also O'Hagan, 1993).

Three studies which examined the effects of maltreatment on language development and school performance all found that neglected children achieved significantly lower scores than other maltreated children (Allen and Oliver, 1982; Wodarski et al, 1990; Kurtz et al, 1993). A further study covering similar ground (Eckenrode, Laird and Doris, 1993) found that, of the maltreated children studied, neglected children showed the poorest outcomes in academic performance and physically abused children showed the most discipline problems.

Attachment theory, which looks at the interactions between parent and infant, particularly the early bonding process, has been fertile ground for neglect theorising. The concept of 'anxious attachment' which derives from Bowlby's classic work, as applied and developed by Ainsworth (1969), offers a way of understanding the relationships between children and parents in some cases of neglect which has appealed to practitioners. Crittenden for example, has linked early bonding, anxious attachment and neglect from a practitioner's perspective (Crittenden, 1993). One of the common features which has been noted by many observers of dysfunctional families is that the parent seems to be 'psychologically unavailable' to the child. Egeland and Eriksen (1987) explore psychologically unavailable caregiving in their longitudinal survey of high risk children. Of the four maltreatment groups identified, they found that the psychologically unavailable group was particularly devastating to the child's overall development. Ethier, Lacharite and Couture (1995) compare a sample of 'negligent' and 'non-negligent' mothers in an attempt to develop a model of the causation of neglect which uses attachment concepts. They found that the negligent mothers showed extreme levels of stress and high levels of depression (which were interlinked) but found that the evidence for a link between this and childhood events was less clear.

Rohner (1986) similarly developed his parental acceptance-rejection theory (which derives from ideas on attachment) and attempted to demonstrate cross culturally valid generalisations about parent child relationships and their implications for child development. Bolton (1983) looked at what happens when bonding fails and built up a clinical theory of maltreatment which he calls 'family resource theory'.

Finally, there has been a small but significant number of studies which look at neglect within the context of child care and parenting in general. Adcock and White (1985) edited the book 'Good Enough Parenting' following an inter-disciplinary seminar. It embodies a degree of professional consensus enabling social workers to define neglect as parenting which is not good enough in certain key respects. Jenner (1992) applies this approach to the child protection arena in her examination of the assessment and treatment of parenting skills and deficits. In considering the effects of neglect on children Crouch and Milner (1993) emphasise the importance of adopting a developmental perspective. What is appropriate in terms of supervision for an infant, for example, is not adequate for a toddler. At a more populist level Leach has advocated the importance of child centred parenting for a number of years (Leach, 1994). Although she does not address directly the issue of child neglect, she builds up a persuasive and sustained argument that children need to be given greater priority in our society and that child care should be seen as a valuable and rewarding task.

If a study by Pitcairn et al (1993) proves to be typical of the way in which thinking about child protection is moving then there may be a trend back towards looking at good enough parenting. Although the study is about evaluating parenting in child physical abuse its application to child neglect would appear to be even more pertinent. The concluding section seems to exemplify a balanced and rational approach to assessment in child protection:

"The majority of routine referrals for child protection, within this study at least, seem to reflect social and family problems rather than cases of serious injury to the child. Child injury is the symptom of a much larger underlying problem within the parent-child relationship, as evidenced by the behavioural disturbance of the children. Professional evaluation, to be fully effective, needs to concentrate not only on the pattern of injury to the child but also on the daily approach to child care and control within the family." (Pitcairn et al, 1993, p88)

Sociological research

Sociologists have generally taken little interest in child neglect per se; the sociological literature around neglect is therefore less focused and more diffuse. This is not surprising given the historical preoccupation of the discipline with broader social structural issues. Corby (1993) gives a useful overview of sociology's contribution to our understanding of child abuse and neglect. He warns against hasty and ill-considered attempts to apply social theory to social work and says that social workers looking to sociologists for indicators for practice are likely to be disappointed. For the practitioner the discipline of sociology is invaluable as a way of locating the problem of child maltreatment in its wider societal context. Sociological approaches are also helpful in directing attention towards the social processes which define child neglect as a social problem which demands a public response.

Most of the work done by sociologists adopts a broad brush approach with little detail on neglect. For example there is a whole tradition of sociological and quasi-sociological research which looks at family and child rearing in the context of community life. Although it does not address neglect directly, it examines parental behaviour over such issues as supervision and leaving children alone, which would be relevant to concepts of neglect (Newson and Newson, 1970, 1978; West and Farrington, 1977; Wilson, 1980; Creighton and Russell, 1995). Although this work has undoubted implications for our understanding of child neglect this body of literature falls outside the scope of this review. The sociological literature referred to below, although few studies address neglect directly, raises issues about societal definitions of and response to child maltreatment which are particularly salient to neglect since this is the area which most strongly impinges on cultural expectations about childrearing and the responsibilities of the family vis a vis the state. Sociological approaches may be ranked in terms of their level of generality, from the highly abstract and theoretical to the more specific and empirical (see Figure 1).

The social construction of neglect

A number of studies examine the *politics of child abuse and neglect*. At the most general level it is obviously true that the neglect of children is not a new phenomenon. Corby argues that the social work profession , being activist and present-oriented, has a very weak sense of history (Corby, 1993); therefore the historical dimension is often missing. Work on the recent political history of the problem of child abuse has, however, to some extent restored the balance. Corby points out that what has changed over time is not so much the abuse and neglect of children in itself, but rather the way in which the problem has been perceived and defined, what could be called the 'social construction' of the problem. The deconstruction of child abuse appears to have become a popular enterprise among academics with a sociological bent and there is no shortage of material which looks at child abuse in this way.

Stainton-Rogers and Stainton-Rogers (1989) use a form of discourse analysis to identify different 'accounts' of child abuse. Subjects were asked to rank 80 statements about child abuse by sorting them in a grid ranging from strongest agreement to strongest disagreement. They found that this is an area of real controversy. There were diverse and divergent understandings of child abuse with no social, or even expert, consensus.

In his discussion of the results of a major empirical study of child protection in Australia, Thorpe asserts that the 'epistemological frame' created by the expression child abuse leads to parents being pathologised (Thorpe, 1994). Child protection language and statistics tend to misrepresent the phenomenon by decontextualising it thus: 'that which does not conform to standard middle class patriarchal child rearing norms is represented as 'at risk' of abuse or neglect' (p202).

Loney (1989) argues that more attention needs to be paid to the social context of child abuse and criticises the dominant disease model. He says:

"child abuse is constructed in a way which is ultimately reassuring ... framed in terms of the 'sick' behaviour of deviant individuals and families or the competence of social workers. The debate about child abuse is taken out of the realm of politics and placed in the hands of the experts." (p88)

Pfohl (1977) in a ground-breaking article adopted a labelling perspective from the sociology of deviance to examine child abuse. He gives an elegant and masterly analysis of the 'discovery' of child abuse in which he points out the critical role of the medical speciality of paediatric radiology which 'saw' physical abuse for the first time. Pfohl explains how Kempe and his colleagues publicised the problem through the use of the powerful label 'the Battered Baby Syndrome' (Kempe et al, 1962). Pfohl writes:

"discovered by the radiologists, substantiated by their colleagues and distributed by the media the label was becoming widespread." (Pfohl, 1977, p320)

Parton, whose recent work addresses neglect more specifically, also uses the labelling perspective, looking at the way in which child abuse in the United Kingdom came to be recognised as a social problem demanding an institutional response, (Parton 1979). He later developed this analysis and built it into a powerful critique of conventional wisdom in child protection (Parton, 1985). Parton takes issue with what he feels is an excessive preoccupation with individual pathology in child abuse thinking, arguing that the traditional concentration on dangerous individuals fails to allow for the significance of dangerous conditions (Parton and Parton, 1989). In a critical appraisal of the Beckford Report (Parton, 1986) he again criticises the disease model of child abuse (namely the concept that abuse is a disease whose cause is the parent and whose victim is the child). The basis of his critique is that child abuse and neglect are not medical problems susceptible to clinical solutions, they are social problems with important economic and political aspects. Parton applies a sociological analysis to neglect in particular (Parton, 1995). He argues that a legalistic, investigatory response is inappropriate in the majority of cases referred for neglect and that a more welfare-oriented preventative approach is required. Wolock and Horowitz (1984) also apply the 'social problems' perspective to neglect arguing that the dominant definition of child maltreatment as child abuse has led to the downgrading of neglect (see also Tomison, 1995).

In exploring *perceptions of abuse and neglect*, several studies have used 'vignettes' describing child mistreatment to examine professional and non-professional judgements on the nature and seriousness of case examples. Several of these give a rather different picture of the degree of social consensus about child maltreatment. Giovannoni and Becerra (1979) report results of an opinion survey of American professionals about the definition of child abuse. The subjects - lawyers, social workers, police and paediatricians - were asked to rank a series of vignettes illustrating different aspects of child maltreatment: the researchers found a large degree of consensus. They report an 'amazing similarity' in judgements as to the relative seriousness of different kinds of mistreatment. In a similar survey of members of the general public they found that community members saw most kinds of mistreatment as more serious than the professional group. Interestingly, black and Hispanic respondents showed greater concern than other ethnic groups, as did those of lower socio-economic status (see Rose and Meezan, 1996 for a more recent study exploring differing perceptions of neglect). This raises a number of questions about the validity of middle class professionals (and researchers') assumptions about child rearing norms and patterns in different social groups.

Craft and Staudt (1991) used the vignette methodology to compare reporting of child neglect in urban and rural communities. Again, the results showed a large degree of consensus, there being few differences between rural and urban respondents. Ringwalt and Caye (1989) looked at the effect of demographic factors on the general public's perception of neglect using the same methodology. They found that gender was the most strongly associated factor, with women being more likely to rank ambiguous scenarios as severe. The respondents' socio-economic status was only marginally associated to perceptions of severity, as was race, with black people marginally more likely to rate ambiguous scenarios as neglectful than white people.

Saunders, Nelson and Landsman (1993) studied 182 families referred to a child protection agency for neglect in Pittsburgh. They found, in spite of a popular belief that neglect is more common in the African American community, there was no significant difference in the incidence of neglect in the African American population as compared with Caucasian families. They concluded that black families, being substantially poorer than white families, have learned to cope with conditions of severe economic deprivation.

These American studies receive support from a similar, smaller-scale study in the United Kingdom which looked at health visitors' and social workers' definitions of child maltreatment (Fox and Dingwall 1985). This also found clear agreement about the relative seriousness of the incidents described.

Neglectful families or neglectful societies?

The sociological literature touches on three important dimensions which have a complex relationship with each other and with the problem of child neglect. These are *poverty, ethnicity and gender*. Any serious attempt at a sociological understanding of neglect needs to take account of these dimensions.

Research on *poverty* in the UK has not usually been conducted with a child care (certainly not a child protection) orientation. Much of the literature on poverty, for example Oppenheim (1993) and Kumar (1993), or on housing, such as Furley (1989), is ignored by child protection academics and practitioners. Holman is an exception, urging the social work world to take seriously the implications of research on poverty (Holman, 1994). Similarly, Baldwin and Spencer (1993) analyse British statistics on poverty, deprivation and child abuse, pointing out some specific links with neglect. They advocate a shift away from interventions targeted at 'high risk' families and towards community wide preventive strategies. From a medical perspective Wynne attempts to address these multiple connections and shows clearly how neglect is linked with deprivation and broad child health issues (Hobbs, Hanks and Wynne, 1993).

The few British studies contrasts with the situation in the USA, where many researchers have noted the strong association between poverty and child neglect, (Daro, 1988; Pelton, 1991; Sedlak, 1993). Some studies, Polansky's pioneering work for example, have taken the income factor into account in the design of their research, in this way attempting to separate out the effects of poverty from issues around child care, Polansky et al (1981). However attempts at disentangling neglect and poverty are often of doubtful value, because in many of these studies neglect is defined, at least partially, in terms of poor material conditions of life for children, so that poor children are neglected children by definition.

Tracey, Green and Bremseth (1993) examine data from a random sample of 500 child welfare cases looking at the need for supportive services and the gaps in service. Their findings underline the importance of environmental stress factors in neglect which was the most frequently reported type of maltreatment. They argue that:

"the families served by child welfare agencies have multiple problems, each interacting with the other. Traditional services target the individual deficits of parents or children with little regard to the surrounding stress factors. Service models that foster supportive environments while building competencies are essential." (p26)

Nelson, Saunders and Landsman (1993) compared newly neglecting families with chronically neglecting families and a control group. They found that the chronic neglect group were significantly more disadvantaged and faced enormous difficulties in supporting more people with the same very low income. Dileonardi establishes that there is undoubtedly a strong relationship between poverty and chronic neglect but is unable to say whether this is a causal link and, if so, in which direction the causal dynamic operates. He concludes:

"families with fewer resources are more likely to be reported for neglecting their children. However, in some cases, the neglect may be characterised as society's neglect of the family rather than simply a family with adequate resources neglecting its children". (Dileonardi, 1993, p557)

Perhaps the question needs reframing. Instead of asking whether poor children are neglected we could ask instead who is responsible for this neglect. Segal and Gustavsson (1990) turn the tables on the conventional wisdom which blames neglectful parents and look instead at 'neglectful social policy'. They argue for a preventive policy agenda which will tackle child poverty at its source. Hewlett (1993), studying 'Child Neglect in Rich Nations' takes a broad view of child neglect, constructing it as a social/political problem rather than an individualistic one:

"the root causes of child neglect in rich nations have to do with new forms of scarcity in both public resources and parental time." (Hewlett, 1993, p2)

Etzioni, a leader of the communitarian movement in the United States, argues that when men and women left to work outside the home they were not adequately replaced. The resulting deficit, which has damaging effects on children and worrying ramifications for society, he characterises as the 'parenting deficit'. Various suggestions are made as to how changed priorities and more family oriented public policy could go some way towards remedying this deficit (Etzioni, 1993).

It has long been acknowledged that there are cultural aspects to the way we define abuse and neglect and a number of studies have considered *ethnicity* in this context. Korbin (1981) pointed out that there is no universal agreement about what is 'normal' or 'desirable' child-rearing practice. The corollary of this is that what is accepted in one culture (eg female circumcision as an initiation rite) may be seen as abusive in others ('female genital mutilation'). This example of cultural relativity is well known and controversial but there are many other less extreme practices which have a value specific to the culture and people who practice it.

Because of the pervasiveness of racism in Western societies there is clearly a danger that the dominant ethnic group will impose their culturally bound definitions of neglect on those from other ethnic backgrounds. In the UK context Thanki (1994) highlights the failure of health and social services to embrace ethnic diversity and argues for positive action informed by the principle of promoting equity.

Channer and Parton (1990) argue that one of the reasons for the over-representation of black children in care is the assumption that mainstream groups have a tendency to try to assimilate other groups to their values. It is for these reasons that Channer and Parton argue for 'ethnically sensitive' practice and Korbin (1993) stresses the need for 'cultural competence'.

As a counter-balance to this emphasis on cultural difference there are a number of American studies, referred to earlier, which demonstrate a high degree of cross-cultural consensus (within a single multi-cultural society) as to what constitutes serious neglect. Giovannoni and Becerra (1979); Ringwalt and Caye (1989) and Saunders, Nelson and Landsman (1993) all found no significant correlation between ethnic origin and definition of neglect. Black and Hispanic respondents tended, if anything, to take a more serious view of the problem of child neglect than did representatives of the majority culture.

Boushel (1994) advocates an integrated approach to anti-oppressive understanding and practice. She offers a framework identifying four factors which have implications for the protective environment of children. These are the value attached to children, the status of women and carers, the social interconnectedness of children and carers and the quality of the protective safety net available.

The relationship between *gender* and neglect has received little attention. In fact, much of the psychologically oriented literature on parent-child interactions and attachment simply assumes that mothers are responsible for child care and development. In some cases this is made explicit, as, for example, when researchers talk about 'neglectful mothers' as though neglect were a property of certain mothers. Parton brings a feminist perspective to bear on women, gender oppression and child abuse (Parton, 1990). However the focus here is predominately on physical and sexual abuse. Indeed it is as a response to the emerging problem of child sexual abuse that the feminist perspective has made its primary contribution in the child protection field.

Some of the literature about neglect alludes to questions of family structure but gender roles are not at the centre of concern. One issue which is very pertinent to the question of neglect is single parent families. Hewlett (1993) points out that rapidly increasing rates of separation and divorce in Western societies have potentially damaging effects on children. Trube-Becker (1976), Codega (1989), Polansky, Gaudin and Kilpatrick (1992c), along with others already mentioned in this survey, make the point specifically that they regard children of single person-headed households as being at significantly greatest risk of suffering neglect. What is less frequently commented upon is the fact that these single person-headed households are overwhelmingly headed by women and that the primary emphasis on women alone as carers creates highly stressful parenting situations (Glachan, 1991). The onerous task of parenting is easier when shared in a mutually agreed way and the isolated mother who has sole responsibility for caring for several children over a prolonged period of time is not in a psychologically healthy situation, (Brown and Harris, 1978).

A recent study is unusual in that it focuses on the father's role in neglecting families (Lacharite, Ethier and Couture, 1996). The study of 48 two parent families (half neglecting and half non-maltreating) explores the mother's perception of her partner and its relation to her adaptation as a parent. They found that, compared to men in non-maltreating families, men in neglecting families were perceived by mothers as being less adequate marital partners, less supportive and more violent. They conclude:

"the results show that the nature of the behaviour of the man towards the mother as she perceives it... significantly influences her capacity to enjoy the relationship with her child, the state of her personal well being as a parent and, to a lesser degree, her capacity to manage her child's behaviour."
(Lacharite, Ethier and Couture, 1996, pp30-31)

Knowles and Mercer (1992) argue from an explicitly feminist and anti-racist viewpoint that practitioners who carry out assessments are negative about one parent families and hold women responsible for the neglect and abuse of children in a way in which fathers are not. Milner (1993) looks at the question as to why it is, in the face of all the evidence that it is fathers who present the greater risk to children, that social workers work with mothers whilst ignoring fathers. She concludes: 'fathering, being ill defined yet of higher status than mothering, is inaccessible to scrutiny in child protection terms' (p52).

Milner suspects that allegations of abuse on the part of fathers are redefined as neglect on the part of mothers. Farmer and Owen (1995) also make reference to the 'gendered nature' of the child protection system and report that in the case of many two parent households assumptions are made that the mother rather than the father figure is responsible for any shortcomings in the children's care.

There is some evidence that females are more sensitive to child care issues than males and are therefore more likely to perceive maltreatment and refer for action (Dukes and Kean, 1989; Ringwalt and Caye, 1989). Boushel (1994) attempts to incorporate a gender analysis into her integrated approach by pointing out the importance of the status of women and carers. There remains however a great deal of scope for researchers employing a feminist perspective to evaluate critically the literature on child neglect.

Responses to neglect

The neglect of children is not simply a matter for academics to debate; it is an urgent and pressing social problem which demands a response. This section of the literature survey looks at material which is concerned with the way in which society responds to neglect and the sorts of solutions to this problem that have been propounded. Firstly the legal framework and policy guidelines for responding to reported child neglect is examined, then evaluative research which looks at current child protection practice is reviewed.

Legal and policy formulations

The way society responds to child neglect through its official child welfare agencies is a matter of law and public policy. Child protection practice is influenced directly by the legal framework within which it operates and by guidance from the Department of Health. Few practising social workers are familiar with current research findings on child neglect, but all should be familiar with the principles of the Children Act and most should have access to Department of Health circulars and guidelines. Indeed, it is often via such official policy formulations that the conclusions of primary research eventually become common currency among practitioners.

The Children Act 1989 provides the legal framework for current child protection practice. The Act was an attempt to enshrine in legislation two contradictory emphases, to be both child-centred and to give parents more rights. This dilemma over achieving a balance between the needs of children and the rights of parents lies at the heart of child protection and the response to it governs the shape of the state's intervention in family life (Frost and Stein, 1989).

'Partnership with Parents' is a principle running through the Act and child protection practitioners are now expected to make greater efforts to work with parents to make families safer for children before resorting to removing children into care. Parents' rights, now expressed as 'responsibilities', become considerably stronger. Even when the parents are shown to have caused 'significant harm', the court must still be satisfied, in the light of the plans presented to it, that making a care order will be better for the child than making no order at all, (Christopherson, 1993).

Under the Children Act 'significant harm' is now the sole ground available for making a care or supervision order. Establishing 'significant harm' thus becomes an essential prerequisite for statutory intervention. Section 31(10) addresses the issue of how to measure significant harm as follows:

"Where the question of whether harm suffered by a child is significant turns on the child's health or development, his health or development shall be compared with that which would reasonably be expected of a similar child".

The difficulty here is that 'health or development' are such broad terms and comparisons with another 'similar child' are so problematic that it seems likely that there will be less recourse, in neglect cases, to the law. Given the problems inherent in defining neglect, the task of establishing to the satisfaction of the courts that significant harm is being suffered by a neglected child is likely to prove overwhelming (Lyon, 1989). There is a growing literature on significant harm (see for example Murphy-Berman, 1994), but what is missing is the application of this concept to neglect cases. Stevenson refers to the 'culture of diffidence' around neglect which, she maintains, hinders social workers from intervening in families even when there are clear grounds for doing so (Stevenson, 1996).

Another interesting aspect of the Children Act in relation to neglect is its provision for 'children in need'. The Act imposes on local authorities the duty to promote the welfare of 'children in need' and to promote the upbringing of such children by their families, (Christopherson, 1993). This preventive thrust of the Act has been welcomed by practitioners, although their welcome is tempered by scepticism about whether the requisite resources will be forthcoming. Because of the priorities of the child protection system in the United Kingdom 'children at risk' are more likely to get a service than 'children in need'. Yet many children who are neglected (in the broad sense of the word), but not registered, are undoubtedly children in need of a service. Ironically these children may get nothing at all until their family situation reaches crisis point and a child protection intervention becomes necessary, (Francis, 1994). Recent research sponsored by the Department of Health (Department of Health, 1995) expresses concern that too many children may be being drawn into the child protection system and similar fears have been expressed in the USA and Australia (see Besharov, 1985; Thorpe, 1994). Farmer and Owen (1995) state:

"some of the children who were drawn into the child protection system would have been better served if they had been treated as 'children in need' under Section 17 of the Children Act. This applied to cases where vulnerable mothers were trying to cope with demanding children in impoverished circumstances and where the issue was poor parental care rather than danger to the child." (pp327-8)

The system for responding to child abuse and neglect was put into place during the mid-1970s following the Maria Colwell case. The then Department of Health and Social Security issued a series of circulars and letters establishing the basis of the current child protection system. This consisted of Area Review Committees, now called Area Child Protection Committees (ACPCs), multi disciplinary committees with responsibility for the management of child protection in their area and the register of children non accidentally injured, now the child protection register. One of the major tasks of ACPCs is to devise and implement local inter-agency procedures for responding to child abuse and neglect. Some ACPCs have set up working parties with the specific remit of devising strategies and procedures for responding to neglect.

ACPCs have been assisted in their tasks by voluminous guidance from the Department of Health. This guidance does not have the status of law in that ACPCs cannot be compelled to follow it, but few would be willing to take the risk of ignoring it. The 1980 DHSS circular 'Child Abuse: Central Register Systems' (Department of Health and Social Security, 1980) outlined four categories of abuse or risk of abuse which could lead to inclusion on the child abuse register: physical injury, physical neglect, failure to thrive incorporated with emotional abuse, and living in the same household as a person who has been convicted of a 'Schedule 1' offence against children.

Since 1980 the categories of abuse have been constructed in slightly different forms, and, most notably, sexual abuse has been added to the list. Neglect however has always been present even if it has not had much prominence. There is some evidence that a category of 'grave concern' was used as a catch-all category for children who were felt to be at risk in some non-specific way. It seems that many neglected children may have been registered in this category. When the category of 'grave concern' was removed from the child protection register in Newham, for example, the list was reduced from 400 to 50; most of those removed were neglect cases (Francis, 1994).

'Working Together under the Children Act' (Home Office et al, 1991) contains the most recent guidance on the subject, together with a definition which summarises the official view of neglect:

"Neglect: The persistent or severe neglect of a child, or the failure to protect a child from exposure to any kind of danger, including cold or starvation, or extreme failure to carry out important aspects of care, resulting in the significant impairment of the child's health or development, including non-organic failure to thrive." (Home Office et al, 1991 p48)

Virtually no other official child protection guidance which relates specifically to neglect has been found in the course of this search of the literature. One exception is the Department of Health report 'Protecting Children: A Guide for Social Workers Undertaking a Comprehensive Assessment' (Department of Health and Social Security and Welsh Office, 1988). This does refer to the particular difficulties involved in assessing neglect and advises social workers:

"neglect rarely comes to the attention of social workers through a precipitating incident. Social workers often have lengthy involvements with chronically neglecting parents but find it difficult to make judgements about the standards of parental care and the effect these can have on the child's safety and development...The neglected child requires the same structured and rigorous approach to assessment and treatment as any other abused child" (p7)

It has often been noted that inquiries into child deaths have had a disproportionate influence on child protection policy in the United Kingdom. Parton (1994) complains that policy and practice agendas have been driven by cases which are seen to have gone wrong and that therefore the system is 'rear end led'. Stevenson makes the same point by a humorous comparison: 'it's like judging the Health Service by a visit to the mortuary!' (Stevenson, 1994). Perhaps one of the reasons why neglect has received so little official attention is because very few child deaths appear to have been the result of neglect alone. Exceptions to this general rule would be Lester Chapman, Malcom Page (Department of Health and Social Security, 1982), Heidi Koseda (Department of Health, 1991) and more recently, 'Paul' (Bridge Child Care Consultancy, 1995). However chronic child neglect is identified by Reder and colleagues as being one of the principal features of child abuse tragedies (Reder, Duncan and Gray, 1993) and it is hard to imagine a child death where concerns around neglect would not arise.

It may be, however, that neglect is belatedly coming to the fore following the death of a child in Islington. The review into this child death was conducted by the Bridge Child Care Consultancy (1995) and the report argues strongly for a review of professional perceptions in relation to recognition and effects of neglect. It calls for more guidance including ways in which instances of neglect may be quantified. Shortcomings in inter-agency communication are highlighted, plus the danger created by a style of intervention based on the perception of the tragic subject and his family as being 'in need' rather than 'at risk'. This conclusion is diametrically opposite to conclusions of recent research cited earlier in this survey and illustrates how the elastic concepts of 'in need' and 'at risk' overlap.

Research in child protection practice

Some research on child protection practice has focused on the *identification and assessment of neglect* by practitioners in varying fields. Polansky is one of the few researchers who has attempted to operationalise his definition of child neglect. He does this with a combination of instruments: the 'Child Well Being Scales' and the 'Maternal Characteristics Scale' (Polansky, Gaudin and Kilpatrick, 1992a; 1992b). Following a field trial of these instruments Polansky concluded that scales do discriminate effectively between neglectful and non-neglectful families. The Childhood Level of Living Scales are available for practitioners in the United Kingdom but, aside from their American flavour, they embody certain cultural and class assumptions which may limit their usefulness in the British context.

In what is described as a 'handbook for practitioners' Stein and Rzepnicki (1983) give some helpful advice concerning the assessment of physical abuse and neglect. Using a systemic model of decision-making they guide the practitioner through the process of determining whether there is credible evidence of abuse or neglect. Neglect is broken into sub-categories including: abandonment, lack of supervision, medical neglect, malnutrition, shelter neglect, clothing neglect and educational neglect.

Attempts have been made by British social workers to devise appropriate instruments to measure neglect and one result is the 'Scale of Parental Caregiving' described by Minty and Pattinson (1994). This scale is in the form of a questionnaire which looks at both physical and emotional categories. Use of the instrument confirmed that, among families referred to an NSPCC child protection team, there were strong associations between physical and emotional neglect. Minty and Pattinson conclude that neglect is a generic category with a definite emotional component rather than being simply a matter of poverty, dirt and poor material conditions.

An identical desire to develop a more systematic and rigorous scale for measuring neglect motivated Srivastava in his work on the 'Graded Care Profile' (Srivastava and Polnay, 1997). This scale is loosely based on Maslow's hierarchy of needs and has the advantage of being multi-dimensional, relatively non-intrusive and easy to administer. The scale has been piloted and is currently being field tested.

Savage (1994) conducted a comparative study of neglecting and non-neglecting families in order to ascertain whether it is possible to observe early indicators of neglect. She concluded that indicators of neglect were found to be present in the neglecting sample and that therefore neglect may be assumed to be predictable. Two checklists are offered for use by health visitors, one containing indicators of neglect (the most prominent with respect to the child being lack of stimulation) and one containing characteristics of neglecting families.

There is a growing body of research which looks at *the operation of the child protection system* in responding to the problem of child abuse and neglect. It is concerned with questions such as: why are some children registered and others not? What factors influence decision-making in child protection? What accounts for the variation in numbers of children on the child protection registers across different authorities? What do 'consumers' think about the child protection services they receive? etc. These studies tend to be empirical in their approach and they involve analysis of quantitative data from official statistics and qualitative data from surveys, questionnaires, and interviews with practitioners. A number of studies have focused on the operation of the child protection system; some including both abuse and neglect and others on the identification and assessment of neglect.

Corby and Mills (1986) examine the operation of the child protection system in one metropolitan borough in the early 1980s. They observed 55 child protection case conferences and found that explicit criteria were rarely used for deciding whether or not children were registered. In fact they expressed concern that the issue of registration had a tendency to become the central concern of case conference, rather than risk to the child. They argued that case conference should have a more explicit focus on risk and should make more efforts to ensure that resources appropriate to the degree of risk be made available.

The 'rule of optimism', which has frequently been invoked in the attempt to explain dangerous social work practice, is derived from a long term study of agency decision-making in child abuse and neglect from 1977-1983 (Dingwall, 1989). In reporting the conclusions of this study Dingwall formulated his 'rule of optimism' theory, namely: 'in a situation of uncertainty child protection workers should favour the interpretation of signs and symptoms which least stigmatises the parents' (p162). This theory, which was a response to the observation that relatively few cases were defined as abuse or neglect, generated a great deal of controversy but may go some way to explaining why fewer neglect cases enter the system.

Packman and Randall (1989) were also concerned with the way the child protection system actually works. In their study of decision-making at the gateway to care they conclude:

"What was apparent was that signs of physical injury were much easier to detect and demonstrate than the more subtle but no less damaging forms of neglect and emotional deprivation or abuse, from which many were perceived to suffer. The visibility of physical harm was sometimes used, therefore, as a convenient peg on which to hang registration, when concerns for the child's well being were much wider and more complex." (Packman and Randall, 1989, p94)

This implies that a proportion of children who are registered under the category of physical abuse are the subject of equally valid concerns with respect to neglect.

Miller, Fisher and Sinclair (1993, 1995) looked at outcomes of referrals for child abuse in an English social services department. They found large variations in outcome among the 817 referrals they followed. These variations, as well as being connected to the nature of the cases themselves, were also significantly associated to 'accidental' factors such as who makes the referral, which social services team they refer to, and who chairs the case conference. Their second study, based on a postal survey of 123 cases, found that, of the four categories of abuse identified, neglect cases were strikingly different in that the registration rate for neglect cases was 100%. This they feel is likely to be due to the fact that neglect cases are frequently bought to case conference as a last resort after considerable professional input and as a response to mounting pressure from agencies. In other words, because the child protection system is more sensitive to physical and sexual assaults on children, only the more severe cases of neglect get to case conference.

In an attempt to find out how different children on the Child Protection Register are from other children, Campbell developed a checklist of 118 family and personality factors thought to be associated with child abuse and neglect, including a replication of Polansky's Maternal Characteristics Scale, said to be a predictor of neglecting mothers. The measure was applied to 25 families attending a local authority's family centres. The children of some of these families were registered and others not. The scores of registered families were compared with those of control families and few differences were noted, either for maltreatment in general or for neglect. Campbell concludes that, either there is little difference between the characteristics of abusing and non-abusing families, or that the process of registration is determined by other factors not solely related to the characteristics of the families under consideration (Campbell, 1991).

Two American studies looking at the operation of the child protection system have interesting conclusions relating to neglect. Alter (1985) looks at decision-making in cases of child neglect using an analogue study of factors that influence child protection workers at the earliest stage of intervention. Contrary to expectation, she found considerable agreement in this decision-making. Ards and Harrell (1993) looked at discrepancies between cases known to child protection agencies and those known to professionals who regularly have contact with children, like teachers, social workers, health professionals etc. One of the major findings was that there is a hierarchy of awareness in operation, with sexual abuse at the top, followed by physical abuse, followed by neglect. Neglect is therefore viewed as being less serious as compared with other forms of maltreatment.

In her study of the impact of child protection interventions on parents, Farmer looked at areas of agreement and disagreement between social workers and parents and children in a typical cross-section of cases (Farmer, 1993). She found that neglect cases tended to have higher levels of disagreement, reporting that: 'parents defended the way they were bringing up their children and hotly disputed the view of the case conference that they were neglectful or emotionally abusive parents' (p51). The implication is clearly that, in terms of working in partnership with parents, neglect cases may present greater challenges to the practitioner.

In a major empirical study of child protection practice in Western Australia (with a comparative study in a Welsh agency), Thorpe undertook a detailed analysis of 325 'substantiated cases' (Thorpe, 1994). This research is unusual in that it is a 100% sample and concentrates on the 'typical' and 'mundane' work done by child protection agencies rather than on a selection of high risk cases. Thorpe's research is based on a computerised child protection database and focuses on outcomes as described in case files. He found that only about 10% of the children drawn in to the child protection system were victims of serious neglect, physical or sexual assaults. The majority of child protection matters were dealt with by investigation and some degree of admonishment. Thorpe is concerned at the over representation of poor and disadvantaged people, single parent families and Aboriginal people amongst service users.

Similar themes emerge from the Department of Health sponsored research on child protection practice in the United Kingdom. Farmer and Owen (1995) advocate the diversion of less serious cases away from the child protection system, as do Gibbons, Conroy and Bell, (1995) who found that only one case out of seven initially referred was eventually registered at case conference. They recommend a shift of emphasis away from investigations and towards more effective post conference services within an inter-agency framework.

Summary and conclusions

The first major problem identified by this survey of the literature is the problem of scope and definition. Neglect is such a large, loosely defined category that almost anything that has been written about child development has implications for our understanding of neglect. There is so much potentially useful material that the researcher is at a loss to know where to start and when to stop. Parameters therefore have to be set in place which necessarily restrict both the scope of the study and the extent to which its findings may be generalised. Further confusion is caused by the fact that child abuse in general and neglect in particular does not fall within the province of any particular discipline, and therefore the literature is fragmented and lacks a unifying perspective.

The second, complementary, problem is the dearth of literature, particularly British literature, specifically on neglect. 'Messages from Research', for example, gives an overview of 20 research studies in the field of child protection (Department of Health, 1995). Of these, eight have a specific focus on child sexual abuse, three on physical maltreatment but there are none focusing on child neglect. Studies looking at child abuse in general include neglect as a category of maltreatment, but there is a distinct shortage of specific material on neglect and emotional abuse as compared to that available on sexual and physical abuse. The vast majority of books, articles and papers produced by the 'child abuse industry', both here and in the United States are concerned with physical abuse and sexual abuse rather than neglect, which is very much the 'poor relation', having a lower profile both academically and among practitioners. Work that has been done on 'child maltreatment' in a generic sense also tends to downgrade neglect. One gets the impression in some studies that neglect is little more than an afterthought, an appendix attached to the main body of work in the interests of comprehensiveness! (Tomison, 1995).

A large proportion of the studies identified in this literature survey are American. Because definitions of neglect are culturally informed the American domination of the literature presents problems for the researcher in the United Kingdom. American research findings may not be replicated in the United Kingdom and, in any event, both the child protection system and the preoccupations of British researchers are different from those across the Atlantic. The physical sciences may speak an international language but social scientists face tremendous problems of translation and interpretation. Great care must therefore be exercised in the way in which American research is used by practitioners in the United Kingdom.

For the purposes of this survey the literature search has been limited by looking at neglect as a sub-category of the larger field of 'child abuse and neglect'. Given a primary child protection orientation this coupling of neglect with child abuse is inevitable, yet it leads to enormous problems. Child abuse seems to be almost infinitely elastic as a category and has expanded tremendously over the years. Hallett is one writer who questions its continuing usefulness:

"There has been a widening of the term child abuse from the 'battered babies' of the 1960s through emotional abuse and neglect to sexual abuse and organised and ritualistic abuse. Yet, as the behaviours associated with the term child abuse expand, we have to ask: is such a wide catch-all term helpful in understanding causation, consequences for the child, possible interventions and preventative strategies, and do professionals share understandings in these matters? The changing term child abuse seems ripe for disaggregation" (Hallett, 1993, p142)

Stevenson (1996), arguing that the time is right for a reappraisal of neglect, urges child protection workers to think across the different categories of abuse and neglect, recognising how much they overlap. Iwaniec makes a similar point. Summing up over twenty years of practice, teaching and research she says:

"After many years of professional involvement in working with emotionally abused and neglected children and their families the author became convinced that the term 'maltreatment' is the most appropriate to describe all forms of child abuse and neglect" (Iwaniec, 1995, p184).

The final and most serious gap in the literature is the almost total absence of social work theory on neglect. By social work theory is meant theoretical approaches developed by social workers as social workers, rather than theoretical approaches from various eclectic sources which social work practitioners happen to find useful. This may partly be explained by the fact that social work as an academic discipline is still in its infancy. It is also due to some confusion, at the theoretical level, as to where social work locates itself in the academic spectrum and what distinctive knowledge base the profession has.

In the distinction between theory and practice, it is very clear where social work locates itself. Social work practice is largely constrained by the official legal and policy formulations of the day and, to a lesser extent, by the findings of evaluative research into current child protection practice. The literature that has come out of the discipline of social work per se tends to be practice-oriented and limited in its theoretical scope. This is probably no more true of neglect than it is of other social work issues but, because neglect is such a challenging concept at a theoretical level, this lack of theory is critical. The belated recognition of neglect is, all too often, followed by intense pressure to 'do something about it'. In this context the scope for thoughtful, reflective, evidence-based social work practice is severely limited.

3 Practitioners' definitions of neglect

Introduction

The literature review indicated that the concept of child neglect is far from being a simple or unitary one. Different disciplines come at the subject from different angles and bring with them their own particular orientations. At the theoretical level there does not appear to be a consensus as to the nature of the phenomenon, its causation and its consequences. Moreover, attention has been directed at the way in which child neglect is socially constructed and may therefore mean different things to different people. Similarly, and not surprisingly, at the level of practice there is diffidence and uncertainty about intervention. Although some previous research had used measurement scales to assess neglect (eg Minty and Pattinson, 1994) the literature review raised questions about whether scales to measure neglect would run the risk of being either too simplistic to be of much value or too complicated and intrusive to put into operation.

Linked to this practical problem is another challenging theoretical problem namely: what is it that neglect scales are to measure? There are aspects of child development which are relatively easy to measure and evaluate, such as growth, but other aspects of a child's welfare are less accessible. How, for instance, do you measure a child's emotional well-being? Yet it is precisely those emotional aspects of a child's experience within the family setting which researchers are increasingly regarding as being fundamental to child maltreatment (Department of Health, 1995).

It was these practical and theoretical problems which directed the search for a way of incorporating the views of child protection professionals into the research design. Professional judgements about child welfare are intrinsic to any assessment of child neglect. The professionals in their routine practice have the responsibility of defining what is and what is not neglect and their opinions about what child neglect looks and feels like are crucial.

The research question therefore evolved from: 'how can neglect be measured?' to the more modest: 'what do practitioners think about neglect and how does this influence the child protection process?'. The research looks at the processes whereby certain families with problems become defined as 'neglect cases', focusing on the way child protection professionals define neglect in practice.

The research design

The design was implemented in two phases. A workshop was held for child protection practitioners from the various agencies making up the Area Child Protection Committee of a Metropolitan Borough. Participants agreed to undertake a number of exercises aimed at gathering information about their opinions on child neglect. Two of these exercises were completed on an individual basis, the others were group exercises undertaken by inter-agency focus groups. The data collected from the workshop was analysed and tabulated, then used to develop a schema for examining the case material.

In the second stage of the project a sample of 20 cases currently registered in the category of neglect was taken from the same authority's child protection register. The keyworkers for these cases were interviewed by the researcher using a semi-structured interview schedule. Data collected from the keyworker interviews was analysed by the researcher who was looking for common themes relating to the ways in which neglect is defined in practice. Fieldwork was carried out in 1994/95:

The practitioners' workshop

In the workshop participants completed two individual exercises. One required them to construct a personal definition of neglect and the other required them to complete a questionnaire about a series of case scenarios or vignettes. Sample response forms for both of these exercises are contained in the Appendix. The exercise on definitions generated qualitative data which was subsequently analysed by the researcher by looking for keywords and themes. The vignette exercise generated more quantitative data which was subjected to a simple statistical analysis.

Focus group discussions

As a methodology focus groups are distinguished from the broader category of group interviews by the explicit use of group interactions as research data (Kitzinger, 1994). Group processes therefore are of interest as well as the content of the data produced. Focus groups have been developed in relation to marketing, communications and media research (Morgan, 1993), and, in the human sciences, have proved to be particularly useful in eliciting information about sensitive subjects like sexual health (Nix, Pasteur and Servance, 1988).

Inter agency focus groups were used in the workshop to gather opinions from child protection practitioners for a number of reasons. Firstly, child protection is (or should be) a collaborative enterprise. The nature of the child protection process lends itself to an approach which takes seriously the interactions between people and group processes. Secondly, child protection is an area where there is considerable disagreement and conflict. Focus groups offer an opportunity for the researcher to observe the ways in which this conflict is dealt with and agreements are negotiated. Thirdly, using focus groups in research is a way of empowering the research participants as the experience of grass roots workers is validated and they are drawn into the research process rather than being kept outside. Finally, focus groups help the lone researcher to avoid 'researcher bias' at the same time as gathering data in a form which is very useful because the data collected is already partially refined by the group.

Survey of neglected children

The sample was a purposive sample (Reid and Smith, 1981). It differed from probability samples in that the question of the extent to which the sample was statistically representative of the population of interest remains unknown. The sample selection was constrained by the purposes of the research and so cases were selected for inclusion because they were thought to be typical of the subject being studied. A copy of the interview schedule used for interviewing the keyworkers, which contained a mixture of closed and open questions, is contained in the Appendix.

Gaining access

In contrast to the experience of many researchers in the field of child abuse and neglect, difficulties with access to confidential information have not been a major obstacle to this research. This is partly due to the current climate of interest in neglect within the authority taking part in the research. It may also be due to a research design which stresses consultation and participation, building on the good inter-agency relationships which already existed in the area.

The co-operation and support of the local Area Child Protection Committee (ACPC) was crucial to the implementation of the research. A number of external factors contributed towards raising the profile of neglect as a child protection issue within the local authority and this undoubtedly made it easier to secure the active support of the ACPC. One of these was the tragic death of a child in a house fire. This child's family was well known to Social Services and the victim himself was registered as being at risk of harm due to neglect. The subsequent enquiry together with a Social Services Inspectorate report both pointed to the need for the Authority to rethink its ways of dealing with neglecting families. One result of these developments was the setting up, in 1993, of an ACPC Subgroup on Neglect which had the specific remit of developing practice guidelines for responding to neglect. NSPCC was represented on this subgroup.

The Neglect Subgroup provided a very useful entry to the full ACPC which gave its formal approval at the outset of the project. The ACPC also gave practical help to the research by paying the cost of the venue for the workshop, thus publicly owning the project.

For the second phase of the research information was required from the local authority's child protection data base. This was again agreed by Social Services senior management and the Register Administrator provided the necessary information. Case material used in the research was annonymised so that no individual child or his/her family could be identified. Participants were assured that no information about their individual practice would be passed on to their line managers and that any practice implications derived from the research would be general in their scope, applying to policies, procedures and systems rather than to individual practitioners.

The workshop

The workshop was held in November 1994 at a large rural conference centre used as a training venue by the local authority. The workshop had been publicised as a 'Child Neglect Workshop' and invitations with response slips sent to all ACPC member agencies. Attendance was good, and the local authority Legal Department was the only member of ACPC which was not represented. There were 33 participants in total. This included 15 people working for a social work agency (most of these being field social workers), 10 people working for health authorities or trusts (most of these being health visitors), five people in education (four teachers or heads and one Education Welfare Officer) and three from police or probation

Table 1 Neglect workshop attendance by agency and gender

Agency	Women	Men	Total
Social work	12	3	15
Health	9	1	10
Education	5	0	5
Police and Probation	2	1	3
Total	**28**	**5**	**33**

The workshop began with a brief introduction from the researcher, stressing that the workshop was for research rather than training purposes and that it was intended to be multi-disciplinary, practice based and participatory. Participants were then introduced to the concept of focus groups and were given assurances about the confidential and independent status of the research. Workshop members were given two individual exercises, with 10 to 15 minutes to do each. They were requested to complete the exercises without consulting with colleagues.

Individual exercises

Definition

Participants were given a blank sheet of paper with the following instruction: 'Define child neglect in your own words. Try to make your definition simple and concise. (This is not an essay question!)'. Participants' responses were limited only by the time available and the size of the paper (A4). The definitions were subsequently analysed by the researcher looking for common themes expressed in keywords and phrases.

Case scenarios

This exercise consisted of a list of 30 possible neglectful situations. Scenarios or 'vignettes' have been used by a number of researchers as a way of elucidating peoples' opinions about the definition of abuse or neglect (Giovannoni and Becerra, 1979; Fox and Dingwall, 1985; Ringwalt and Caye, 1989). The scenarios are obviously highly condensed and have limitations when compared with the complexity of real life situations. However they do have the merit of producing quantitative data which can be analysed in various interesting ways.

The scenarios used in this exercise were developed by Craft and Staudt (1991) who used them in research looking at the reporting and substantiation of child neglect in urban as compared with rural communities in the USA. A few minor changes were made to the case descriptions to make them more appropriate to the British context. They cover issues such as supervision, feeding, clothing, material conditions in the house, parent child interactions, household routines etc (see Appendix for the list of examples and sample response form).

Respondents were asked to answer two questions in respect of each scenario, indicating their answers by placing a tick in the chosen column. The first is whether or not they would refer for a child protection investigation, and has a straight yes or no answer. The second asks the respondent to rank the standard of child care demonstrated on a scale of 0 to 5, where 0 is dangerously neglectful and 5 is adequate or non-neglectful.

In analysing the results the researcher was looking for the degree of agreement or disagreement within the professional community about potentially neglectful situations, and the correspondence between responses about referral and level of child care. It was expected that there would be a positive correlation between seriousness and referral.

The researcher was interested in whether there were significant differences in the responses across agency and gender variables. Any deductions from these results have to take into account the small size of the sample and the fact that the effects of these two variables cannot be separated out.

Results of the 'definitions' exercise

The definitions were analysed by looking for common themes expressed in keywords or phrases. Table 2 lists the most common words used in respondents' definitions. The most common theme was that of a child's basic or primary needs not being met. 'Needs' was the most common keyword, being mentioned by over half of the respondents. Needs were frequently divided into physical and emotional, with social and psychological needs also mentioned.

The second most common keyword was 'care', (mentioned by 13 respondents). The presupposition seemed to be that children are dependent for their well-being and development on adult parent/carers who have a duty to meet these various care needs. This duty is not spelt out but is implicit in phrases like 'failure to recognise' children's needs (five respondents), or 'blind to the child's need' or 'lack of sensitivity' to children's needs. One respondent comments that failure to care may be due either to inability or unwillingness. Neglect there-

Table 2 Keywords used in practitioners' definitions of neglect

	General	Physical	Emotional
Positive	needs care protection development safety	food warmth clothing shelter health medical attention	love affection attention security interest praise education stimulation guidance play
Negative	impaired development danger harm suffering	dirty smelly unwashed failure to thrive	rejected isolated

Base: 33 participants in the workshop exercises

fore is defined as what happens when children fail to receive the care or nurturing that is 'reasonably expected'. Some definitions used 'rights' instead of 'needs', thus giving a stronger and more empowering emphasis.

Many of the definitions specified primary needs and the most common physical needs were food (10 mentions), clothing (7) and shelter (7). The most common emotional needs were love (9) and warmth (9). Also mentioned were affection, attention, support, interest, security and praise. One respondent wrote that neglect is when 'children's ideas, feelings and opinions are ignored'.

Some primary needs were mentioned negatively when, for instance, neglected children were described as being unclean, dirty, smelly, unwashed. They were seen as being persistently rejected and isolated, or 'emotionally fragile' (that is having behaviour problems, tempers, mood swings, difficulty relating to peers). One respondent mentioned 'being subjected to scenes of violence and aggression'.

Another important theme in neglect is supervision and, although this particular keyword was, surprisingly, not used at all, the concept was clearly present. Protection from danger or harm, and safety, figure quite prominently in the responses. Interestingly, 'overprotection' and 'smothering' are also mentioned, which imply a more complex conceptualisation of children' needs than the simple need for love and attention.

Children's medical needs are also mentioned, health and the need for medical attention. Failure to thrive received two mentions, one further qualified as 'non-organic failure to thrive'. Education was recognised to be important, both formally (school attendance) and in the home: stimulation, play, guidance and discipline were all mentioned.

Development was referred to frequently, both as a desired outcome, but also as something that was jeopardised by neglect which was seen as causing suffering, under-achievement, failure to reach potential and impaired development.

The wider context of neglect did not receive much attention though two respondents considered that neglect is relative to other children living in that community, and to social expectations. One respondent acknowledged that responsibility for neglect may not just be at the family level but also at the level of local and central government, and another stated that 'anything that takes away or does not give a child the right to develop and be happy is neglect'. Perhaps the most poignant comment was from the person who said that 'a neglected child does not experience childhood', a sentiment echoed by someone else who wrote about 'unfair levels of responsibility placed on children of tender years'.

Table 3 Practitioners would refer for a child protection investigation

Scenario Number	Scenario	Would refer Yes	No
21	A child suffers from an ongoing illness and is not receiving essential medical care	33	0
6	A child often witnesses his mother being physically abused by his father	32	1
12	An 8 year old child is left at night to baby-sit three younger siblings while the parent works	32	1
27	A child begs for food. The child has not eaten in a day	32	1
10	A 13 year old child does not go to school and the parents do not attempt to intervene	30	3
16	A 5 year old consistently smells of urine. She is isolated at school and her classmates bully her	29	4
4	A primary school age child is expected to prepare his own meals almost daily	29	4
25	Three children in a family are in special education classes and regularly miss one or two days of school a week	28	5
30	A 9 year old child is required to provide the discipline for her younger siblings	28	5
13	A parent was to pick up his/her child from the baby-sitter at 4pm and did not return until the next day. This was the second time this happened	27	6
8	Parents with learning difficulties are unable to rid their infant of nappy rash. The GP is concerned about the baby's health	25	8
5	A 10 year old child goes to school tired every day. She admits to having no set bedtime and sleeps on the living room couch	24	9
17	A child is often ignored when he tries to tell his parent something and is pushed aside when he shows a need for love	24	9
18	A nurse who is a single parent has two children (aged 11 and 2). Her shifts means sometimes leaving the children on their own for a few hours some days. There have never been any problems	24	9
1	A 10 year old girl is home alone from 3.30pm to 6.30pm Mondays to Fridays	24	9
15	A parent leaves an infant in an unlocked car for 15 minutes whilst she is in the supermarket	23	10
22	A parent frequently screams obscenities at the child and the child cries	21	12
26	A 12 year old child is required to do all the housework	21	12
23	A family relies on state benefit and does not spend money wisely, often running out of food by the end of the week	16	17
14	A young mother of 3 children often uses her benefit on non-food items such as beer and cigarettes	15	18
3	A child consistently wears clothing that is ill fitting and in a poor state of repair	13	20
19	A child does not have appropriate toys and the parents make no attempt to obtain them	13	22
28	A primary school child eats lunch at school but has no hot meals at home	11	22
24	A 12 year old child has never been to the dentist	7	26
2	A parent with a drink problem allows their 12 year old child to drink from their beer mug	7	26
7	A parent has not taken care of necessary repairs around the house. There is broken glass on the front doorstep	6	27
9	A child is often seen outside on a cold winter's day with no hat, mittens and only a light jacket	6	27
29	A child does not have a bath for a week at a time	5	28
11	There are no carpets at all in the house	4	29
20	A parent seems not to follow through on threatened punishments and very frequently no action is taken when discipline is required	4	29

Base: 33 participants in the workshop exercises

Case scenarios and referrals

Table 3 shows the results of the case scenario exercise in terms of the answers to the question about referral. The results indicate a great deal of variation in professionals' responses to potentially neglectful situations with consensus at the extremes, but a large area in which there is little agreement. The situation which is regarded by respondents as most extreme (Scenario 21) has 100% agreement to refer. Situations which are regarded as least serious (Scenario 11 and 20) by contrast, have 87% agreement not to refer.

The situations where there is the greatest degree of consensus to refer, tend to be where the issue seems to be most clear cut eg a child's physical health is at risk (Scenario 21), a child witnesses physical abuse (Scenario 6), or a child begs for food (Scenario 27). At the other end of the scale the situations where there is greatest consensus not to refer are a lack of discipline (Scenario 20), no carpets and poor state of house (Scenarios 11 and 7), inappropriate clothes (Scenario 9) and no baths (Scenario 29). All these situations, whilst being matters of concern, would not be grounds, in the opinion of the great majority of respondents, to initiate a child protection investigation. In between these two extremes are situations where professional opinion is divided. The two examples which cause the greatest division are Scenarios 14 and 23, both relating to the management of money in situations of scarcity. All the items relating to supervision and leaving children alone led to marked division of opinion, and Scenario 3 (child consistently has inappropriate clothing) and Scenario 19 (lack of toys) also divide professional opinion. These scenarios get only between 50 and 60% agreement on the question of referral.

Ranking standards of child care

Respondents were asked to make a judgement about the standard of child care on a scale of 0-5, but there are still clearly discernible overall patterns in the responses given. As with the definition exercise, the more extreme the situation is judged to be, the more closely the responses are clustered together. Scenario 21, for example, a child not receiving adequate medical care, has 22 responses in column 0 (dangerously neglectful). In contrast, scenario 26, a mildly worrying situation where a 12 year old child is required to do all the housework, gets a much flatter set of responses spread across the whole scale.

Consensus within the group was higher on which scenarios were dangerous than on which were adequate or safe: of the 30 scenarios, 5 were given a rating of 0 or 1 (the most dangerous) by two thirds or more of the participants. At the other end of the scale, no scenarios received equal consensus on safety, with very few ratings of 5 (the 'safest' score) and only one item (absence of carpets) being scored 5 by more than one third of the group. Only two scenarios achieved two thirds agreement on the two lowest scores.

Interestingly, there was not a straightforward relationship between the decision that a situation should be referred for a child protection enquiry and the assessment of danger or safety. Situations in which children faced immediate and potentially life threatening risk were rated both as dangerous and as meriting a child protection enquiry, but there were many situations where there was a high consensus on referral or non-referral, but little consensus on danger. Table 4 gives examples from each end of the spectrum, and from the centre group. This illustrates some of the dilemmas concerning the boundaries between child welfare, children in need and child protection. The centre group appears to represent situations where there is no immediate risk to safety but practitioners fear that worse could follow. These examples show the way in which a Section 47 enquiry would be used, even though the child was not seen as being at immediate risk of significant harm.

Table 4 Consensus on referral and dangerousness of neglect

Scenario Number	Scenario	Would Refer		0	1	2	3	4	5
		Yes	No	Most dangerous / least dangerous					
Consensus on dangerous situations which would be referred									
21	A child suffers from an ongoing illness and is not receiving essential medical care	33	0	22	4	5	2	0	0
12	An 8 year old child is left at night to baby-sit three younger siblings while the parent works	32	1	21	9	1	1	0	1
Consensus on referral but disagreement on dangerousness									
13	A parent was to pick up his/her child from the baby-sitter at 4pm and did not return until the next day. This was the second time this happened	27	6	4	7	11	9	2	0
25	Three children in a family are in special education classes and regularly miss one or two days of school a week	28	5	0	5	11	8	7	2
30	A 9 year old child is required to provide the discipline for her younger siblings	28	5	3	6	13	6	4	1
Consensus that would not refer and agreement on absence of danger									
11	There are no carpets at all in the house	4	29	0	1	2	4	12	14
24	A 12 year old child has never been to the dentist	7	26	0	2	3	6	20	2

Base : 33 participants in the workshop exercises

Focus group exercises

Participants had been allocated to their groups prior to the Workshop, so that each group would be as varied as possible in terms of agency representation. Because all participants belonged to member agencies of the same ACPC and worked in the same area, some knew each other and had worked alongside one another as colleagues. They were also used to working to the same policies and procedures and would therefore have been influenced to some extent by the culture and ethos of their particular local authority.

Because of the discrepancy between anticipated and actual attendance the four focus groups varied in size from six members to 10 members but they all contained a balance of members from the full cross section of agencies. The gender mix was less even (28 women and five men) but this is indicative of the predominance of women in child care occupations. There were no ethnic minority participants which again reflects the nature and composition of child protection services in the area.

Groups were asked to present their conclusions to the researcher at the end of each session before starting the next task. Each task was defined as loosely as possible and there was no interaction between the groups whilst they were working on their tasks simultaneously. The four focus groups were given identical tasks and every effort was made to create similar environments for each group. The group tasks were deliberately ordered so that there was a logical progression, moving from the most general and least threatening, to a specific focusing on neglect, and finally to the most personal involving sharing feelings provoked in the worker by dealing with child neglect. Groups were given 25 minutes for each exercise.

All the participants in the Workshop were from the local area and many of them knew each other as colleagues or friends; similarly, many of the participants were previously acquainted with the researcher. The effect of this on group processes is difficult to quantify, but it seems reasonable to assume that it allowed the groups to run more smoothly and easily than they would otherwise have done. The danger is that shared assumptions might not have been challenged as fully as possible.

Observations of the groups in operation and comparison of the work they produced indicated that each group developed its own identity and approached the task in a unique way. Yet there was also a remarkable degree of consistency both in the results achieved and in the group processes which led to these results.

The discussions flowed relatively easily and there was a high level of participation by all group members. No one professional group dominated the discussions though social workers, being the largest occupational group, probably made the most individual contributions. The discussions were good humoured throughout and no heated confrontations were observed although some issues were clearly contentious and different points of view were expressed. The tasks generated a great deal of enthusiasm and individuals continued to discuss issues during breaks when the focus groups broke down and people reformed into natural groups.

In making contributions to the discussion participants drew mainly on their own practice rather than on theory. Many of the contributions were prefaced by remarks like: 'I find that...' or 'in my experience...' or 'don't you think that...?'.

The needs of children

For this exercise each focus group was asked to answer the question: 'What are children's needs?'. The group was asked to reach a consensus, which they would record, as to what children need.

The results of this exercise are presented in Table 5. The original words and phrases have been used wherever possible. The order of the items listed in the various groups has been changed to reconcile them across the groups and the generic categories have been added by the researcher. The most striking aspect of these results is the degree of consistency across the four focus groups. Each group listed between 18 and 25 items and nearly all of them correspond with each other, frequently the very same words and phrases are used.

There is complete unanimity on the physical or material needs of children with all four groups agreed that children need food, shelter and warmth. It is when attempts are made to quantify the amount or quality of these items that the controversy begins. That children need an 'adequate diet' and 'appropriate clothing' is understood and agreed by all. Exactly what constitutes an adequate diet and appropriate clothing however is more problematic. Another interesting feature of the results is the priority given to the emotional needs of children. Three out of four focus groups put 'love' at the very top of their list. The emotional needs category can usefully be subdivided into three: esteem, individuality and security. The cluster of responses around independence and individuality show a sophisticated understanding of children's emotional needs which have to do both with attachment and separation. Children's needs obviously change as children grow and mature so that all the needs of children have a developmental character. However, some of the items listed refer specifically to this aspect of children's lives and these have been given the generic category development. Words and phrases like 'opportunities to develop' and 'experiences of life' indicate the importance of children being exposed to new experiences, of being challenged and stretched.

The supervision needs of children are emphasised by the words 'protection' and 'safety'. It is interesting to note that again supervision is not mentioned by name although this is

Table 5 The needs of children - focus groups

	Group 1	Group 2	Group 3	Group 4
Material	food, adequate/ nutritional diet	food	food	
	shelter	shelter	shelter, space/ privacy	shelter, space/ privacy
	warmth	warmth	warmth	warmth
	clean warm clothing	be clean	physical care	clothing
Emotional - Esteem	love	love and affection	love	love, care
		respect	respect, trust	respect
			praise	praise
			encouragement	acceptance/ encouragement
		to be happy		
		able/allowed to show feeling		
Emotional - Individuality	independence	to have independence	independence/ age appropriate	
		to be an individual	rights as an individual	
	freedom of choice	make choices/ decisions	right to say no	giving choices
		have opinion listened to	to be listened to	a voice to be heard
Emotional - Security	discipline/boundaries	guidance/discipline/ boundaries	routine?	consistency boundaries guidance
	structure	security stability	security support	sexuality support
Development	stimulation	stimulation	stimulation	stimulation
		recreation/play	play, pleasure	play
	opportunities	opportunities to develop	opportunities	
	socialisation	to be a child	experiences of life	
Supervision	protection	protection	protection	
			safety	safety
	recognise disturbance	access to professional support		
Social	education in parenting	education	education	education
Human Rights	avoidance of prejudice	not oppressed re disability or gender	truth	a fairer society
	avoidance of prejudice	no racism, sense of cultural identity	cultural identity	
Other	meeting needs	sensitivity to needs	family?	responsible adult care-taker

Base : 33 participants in the workshop exercises

thought to be a key feature of neglect. This highlights the lack of consensus shown in the 'Scenario' exercise on the importance of specific aspects of supervision. The cluster of items around development and protection imply an awareness of the importance of balance in the bringing up of children. The need to be protected has to be weighed against the need for children to explore and have new experiences without the concern for the one overwhelming the other. The need for education and health care are somewhat different in that, in our society at least, they imply some sort of collective provision. They are given the generic category social needs because there is an expectation on society rather than the family to provide for them, or at least to supplement parental provision.

Finally, there were some items listed which are not just relevant to children but relate to all members of society. These have been placed within the generic category human rights because they emphasise that children have rights too. Two of the focus groups, actually made separate lists of rights of children as distinct from needs, but the majority of the items listed in all groups could be construed as either needs or rights. The difference between needs and rights seems to be a matter of association rather than substance. Rights have legal and constitutional implications and clearly belong in the public domain.

Identifying significant features of neglect cases

This exercise was intended to explore factors which child protection professionals think are important in their experiences of dealing with neglecting families. These 'significant features' could be taken to represent a professional consensus on the defining factors of child neglect. Focus groups were given 25 minutes to complete this exercise. Out of the three tasks this is the one which proved most difficult to analyse (Table 6).

These results point to the difficulty of disentangling neglect from other forms of abuse, or indeed from generalised developmental delay, which could itself be the result of a whole host of different factors. Neglect is generally conceptualised as a distinct sub-category within the wider generic category of 'abuse' or 'maltreatment'. It is also differentiated from 'emotional abuse' for registration and therapeutic reasons. Yet the items which have to do with a child's emotional well being are thoroughly interwoven with other items in the focus groups' responses here. Similarly, both the 'symptoms' observed in the child's presentation and behaviour and factors in the parents' personal histories and family functioning could equally be related to physical or sexual abuse. In fact some participants remarked that neglect frequently 'masks' other types of abuse.

If one takes into account these difficulties, the results show a fair degree of consistency. This is particularly evident when the generic categories are looked at as a whole. The largest cluster of responses (32 in all) have to do with the neglected child him or herself. These are 'signs and symptoms' which can be observed, or deduced from observations of the child over time. Whether these factors are cause or effect of neglect is unclear, but this is not surprising since neglect tends to be defined, in a tautological fashion, in terms of its consequences for the neglected child. Some of the items listed are symptoms in the strict medical sense eg 'visible physical injuries' and 'frozen watchfulness', whereas others approximate a medical diagnosis eg 'failure to thrive' and 'developmental delay'. 'Poor hygiene', 'inappropriate clothing' and 'appearing hungry' are simple observations, whereas the responses to do with disturbed behaviour are interpretative in that an association is assumed between neglect and the child's behaviour.

All four focus groups recognise the importance of the parents' own personal histories and the results strongly imply that practitioners perceive a generational aspect to the transmission of neglect. Parents of neglected children present as being poorly equipped to care for their children, showing a lack of sensitivity and responsiveness to their needs, a lack of skill in managing their children's behaviour and a general lack of competence in the practical side of parenting. The emotional deficit in the relationship between parents and children in neglecting families is signalled by the items 'lack of bonding' and 'parent's inability to care/nurture'. Parents who have a substance abuse problem or a mental illness or disability are thought to be over-represented amongst neglecting families.

Family dynamics is referred to in 12 different items and is therefore clearly important in assessment. The items within this group reflect participants' common experience that neglecting families are dysfunctional in some way. Some of the responses refer to processes which may operate in families, such as 'scapegoating', 'unrealistic expectations of child', 'parent's needs before child's needs' and 'violence'. Some items are more general eg 'lack of boundaries' 'dynamics' (presumably unhealthy ones!) and 'dysfunctional

Table 6 Significant features of neglect cases - focus group conclusions

	Group 1	Group 2	Group 3	Group 4
Child	delayed development		developmental delay/language	
	lack of stimulation delayed socialisation			
	behaviour problems	emotional/behavioural difficulties	reported behaviour problems	behaviour problems
	personality changes	withdrawn/subdued aggression	extremes–withdrawn extremes–aggression	
		visible physical injury		
	regression			
		continual minor injuries – unexplained	physical abuse	
		disinhibited/ inappropriate sexuality	sexual abuse	
	frozen awareness	frozen expression		
		poor hygiene		poor hygiene
		hunger – appearing hungry at school		
	failure to thrive	failure to thrive weight gain?	failure to thrive	failure to thrive
	innappropriate medical requests	sickness	repeated hospital attendances	poor health
Parents	parents' experience of being parented			poor parenting of parents
	parents being abused as children		history of neglect/ abuse in parents lives	vulnerable adults
	parents who have experienced the care system			
	parents with substance abuse problems			drink problems/ drugs
	parents with mental illness	disability of parent		
	insensitivity to need – physical/emotional	parents' inability to care/nurture	lack of bonding	
		lack of parental education, poor parenting skills		poor education of parents
		lack of understanding – cause/effect		mismanagement/ prioritisation
Family Dynamics		stress within family		high stress levels
	secondary deviance in children and parents		scapegoating	dynamics
		unrealistic expectations of child	unrealistic expectations of child	
		parents' needs before child's needs		parents needs first
			lack of boundaries	dysfunctional family
Supervision			violence	
		lack of supervision		lack of supervision
			inappropriate carers	
Compliance	availability to agencies	recurrence of problems	documented referrals over period	
	attitude to professionals/ denial	inappropriate medical care	non-complience with medical needs	frequent DNAs
			poor school attendance	poor school attendance
Social		deprivation		deprivation – lower socio–economic groups
	poverty	poverty		poverty
	poor finance			low income – debts
		unemployment – reliance on benefits		
		poor housing/ environment		poor housing
		class/status barriers in recognising signs		
		race/culture diffentials		
		lack of access to services		lack of support services
		breakdown of the community		isolation lack of support

family'. There is a recognition that stress levels in such families are likely to be high.

Once again, supervision has a low profile. 'Lack of supervision' is mentioned by only two groups, another group lists 'inappropriate carers'. Given that supervision is generally regarded as being a key issue in neglect this is perhaps surprising.

One cluster of responses which had not been anticipated is the set which refers to the families' attitudes towards official agencies. These items are given the generic category compliance. Professionals who took part in the workshop clearly feel that neglecting families are resistant, non-compliant and unreliable. The impression given is that these families are regarded as extremely difficult to work with, though whether this is thought to be due to the chaotic, disorganised character of some neglecting families or due to resistance and active denial, is not clear. One group suggests that their 'availability to agencies' is a factor, implying that it is those families which are most closely scrutinised and monitored by professionals which are the most likely to be labelled as 'neglecting' or 'problem families'. This phenomenon has been identified in other studies of child maltreatment (Thorpe, 1994; Department of Health, 1995).

Finally, there is a major set of items (17 in total) which have to do with poverty and deprivation. All the groups bar one record social factors as being significant common features of neglect cases. Here the focus is on deficits within the community rather than the family and professionals acknowledging their agencies' deficiencies in providing respectful and non-oppressive services to neglecting families. The 'breakdown of community' results in the 'isolation' of neglecting families and, for families that are already experiencing the unrelenting pressure of poverty, the task of caring for children becomes even more arduous.

Feelings provoked by working with child neglect

The final exercise was aimed at exploring workers' personal feelings about working with neglecting families. A number of writers on neglect have indicated that such work is very stressful and demanding (Polansky et al, 1981; Moore, 1994) and the researcher was interested in whether participants expressed feelings similar to those which have been identified in previous research, ie feelings of helplessness, despondency and pessimism about the outcome of their interventions.

In this task, practitioners were asked to describe their own feelings about working with child neglect. The combined results are shown in Table 7. The most striking thing about the feelings listed is that they are, almost without exception, negative. The only positive feelings which get a mention are 'sympathy' and 'protective', otherwise it is a picture of unremitting distress and confusion. The potent mixture of sadness, anger and anxiety is remarkably akin to the classical symptoms of depression.

The largest set of responses (18 in total) are to do with sadness/despair and within this category there is a high level of agreement across the groups. The feelings of 'helplessness', 'powerlessness' and 'being overwhelmed' mirror very accurately feelings expressed by parents in neglecting families. This dynamic clearly needs to be recognised by professionals working in such situations as it has the potential to block or hinder constructive change. How are professionals to empower service users if the service user's own sense of helplessness is so contagious that the professional helper feels totally disempowered him/herself?

Anger and frustration are listed by all four groups and there is a greater degree of unanimity in this category than any other. Professionals working with neglecting families need help in learning what to do with their anger otherwise it may be projected back onto the service user ('resentment, irritation, victim-blaming') or else it may be repressed and turn into depression.

Table 7 Feelings provoked by working with neglect - focus group conclusions

	Group 1	Group 2	Group 3	Group 4
Sadness / Despair	sadness	sadness		sadness
	despair		demoralisation	depression
	inadequacy	inadequacy	"it's too late!"	
	helplessness		overwhelmed	powerlessness
	neglect	acceptance	blasé	
		sympathy	pity	pity, sympathy
Anger / Frustration	anger	anger	anger, fury	anger
	frustration	frustration	frustration	frustration
	victim-blaming			resentment/ irritation
Anxiety / Stress			apprehension/ nervousness	anxiety
			"can I go off sick?"	stress, panic
		fear of being blamed		fear
		guilt	guilt	guilt, suspicion
		responsibility		responsibility
Denial / Revusion			revulsion	nausea, disgust
			denial by family and worker	denial
			"I wish I hadn't seen this!"	disbelief
		"passing the buck"	"why didn't someone else do something?"	flight
Professional Confusion		confusion about level of intervention		
		when? – level of urgency	using "bond" as an excuse not to act	
		gut reactions to need – respond to immediate	rise to challenge of environment rather than parents	
		ambiguity regarding regional differentials		
	prejudice	professional rationing – value judgements about need		judgmental
			"can I offer any better? care can damage"	
	disagreement	isolation		
		resources – lack of time and money	"we've no resources"	
Other				protective

Base: 33 practitioners attending the workshop exercises

Child protection is notoriously anxiety-provoking and it is not surprising that there is a cluster of responses concerning anxiety and stress. The potential for anxiety and fear to have a negative effect on workers' own health is not be underestimated and may be related to higher than usual levels of stress-related illness within the occupational groups involved in this type of work. Another negative response to stress is avoidance and this too is well documented in the groups' answers. This category has been given the generic title denial/revulsion. The reaction is often 'Why me?' and workers endeavour, in various ways, to pass on the responsibility to someone else.

Finally there is a large and heterogeneous group of items which have been placed within the generic category professional confusion. Some of these are not, strictly speaking, feelings at all, but are reactions of confusion and self-doubt produced by the ambiguity and complexity of situations faced by child protection professionals. Conscientious workers, anxious to get it right, are acutely aware of the complementary dangers of over-reaction on the one hand and under-reaction on the other. There is a degree of uncertainty about the mandate to intervene in troubled families combined with a scepticism about the alternatives on offer. The possibility that intervention may, in the long run, do more harm than good is perceived as being a real one ('can I offer any better?' 'care can also damage') and produces at best caution and at worst paralysis. In such ambiguous situations the difficulty of making judgements about standards of child care, which may have far reaching implications for the families involved, is compounded by cultural, regional and class differences.

Summary and conclusions

The agencies represented in the Area Child Protection Committee of one local authority were invited to attend a practitioners workshop on child neglect. Thirty three participants from education, police, probation, health and social services carried out a series of group and individual exercises to identify practitioners' perspectives on neglect. The exercises covered: the practitioner's ratings of safe or dangerous 'scenarios' for children; their assessment of children's needs; the decision on when they would refer specific case scenarios for a child protection enquiry, and what characteristics were regarded as significant features of child neglect cases. Finally they were asked to describe their own feelings about working with neglect.

Results showed that while there was a high level of consensus at the extremes, there were substantial areas of disagreement on the seriousness of many potential neglect criteria. Practitioners were united in defining deprivation of basic necessities such as food, warmth and medical care as both neglectful and serious with equal agreement that poor hygiene and discipline would not justify child protection intervention. Issues which had the least agreement were those concerning poor management of money in situations of scarcity, poor supervision of the child and a lack of toys or suitable clothing.

The 'significant features' of neglect cases described by practitioners were analysed and classified. They clustered into responses concerning the child, the parents, caregivers, the family dynamics, the social context, and relationships with the practitioners. Supervision of children again appeared to have a low priority.

A group of items identified as 'compliance', the willingness or ability of the parents/caregivers to work with the practitioners, emerged as key factors in determining practitioners responses to neglect, and the importance of compliance was highlighted because practitioners expressed generally pessimistic feelings about working in neglectful situations. They reported finding this work particularly difficult and having little expectation of success in improving children's or families' situations.

The results of the workshop exercises were used to develop a structured interview schedule for the second stage of the project, reported in the next chapter.

4 Common themes in practitioners' assessment of neglect

The survey

A sample of 20 cases was selected from the local authority Child Protection Register. All were registered in the category of neglect. The Child Protection Register for this Authority contained a total of 265 children (as at March 1994). However, in the category of neglect alone there were only 61 children registered. This sample therefore represents one third of the neglect cases currently registered.

The sample was selected by the researcher from data supplied by the Register Administrator. Criteria for selection were that the registrations should be recent (ie 1993/94), that they should have a different keyworker for each case and that they should preferably be in the pre-school age range. Of the 20 children, 15 children were five years or younger; the others were the next youngest otherwise eligible. Only one child per family could be selected, in order to prevent the results being skewed by siblings from larger families. Where more than one sibling was registered, the youngest was chosen for the sample. The intention was to obtain a sample that would be reasonably representative of neglect cases across the Authority.

The selection was limited to cases with different 'keyworkers' ('keyworker' is the role identified as the co-ordinator of work with the child and family). This was to ensure a widespread geographical distribution of cases, thus avoiding concentrating on individual workers or particular area offices. Individual workers may have particular idiosyncrasies and individual teams may have different 'thresholds of intervention' in neglect cases. In their detailed study of registrations in one English social services department, Miller, Fisher and Sinclair (1993) found that such apparently accidental factors as which team investigates an allegation of child abuse or neglect, or which manager chairs the Case Conference, have a significant bearing on the outcome. In fact the sample included at least one case from each of the seven area teams in the Authority, plus several held by the specialist child protection team. Secondly, interviewing 20 different keyworkers should give a good overall impression of the state of social work opinion in the Local Authority.

The decision to sample cases mainly from the pre-school age range was made because some 35% of the Authority's total registrations for neglect fall within this age group. Failure to thrive also tends to be diagnosed only in babies and younger children and the researcher wanted to include such cases. As a general rule babies and younger children are perceived to be more vulnerable and therefore at greater risk of neglect so it was thought that these cases might give clearer indications of the sorts of situations which give rise to concerns around neglect. Furthermore, health visitors, who are key players with respect to identifying neglect, are more closely involved with pre-school children.

The children

The mean age of the children in the sample was 3.7 years old. Nearly half of the sample were below the age of two, three quarters were five or below. The gender mix was 12 boys and eight girls, and this preponderance of boys over girls was also seen in the total registrations for neglect in the Borough. The ethnic origin of 19 children was White British, and one child was Greek Cypriot in origin. This is also not surprising given the small numbers of people from ethnic minorities who live in the area. Seven of the twenty children were subject to a legal order, mostly care orders or interim care orders.

The data on family structure illustrate the wide diversity of living situations experienced by these children. Less than half of the sample children (eight) lived with both biological parents in a traditional two parent family. Nearly as many (seven) lived in reconstituted families of various sorts, mostly consisting of mother plus a new male partner. Five children lived with their mother in a single parent household, though, of these, one child lived with mother and maternal grandparents and another was cared for alternately by mother and then by father. For all of the sample children their biological mother was a key care giver, whereas fathers, in general, were more peripheral.

The size of the sample children's families were unremarkable, varying from seven siblings to none. Because sample children's families were changing all the time, growing, separating, reforming etc the sample only gave a 'snapshot' impression of the situation at one specific point in time. There did not appear to be any significant pattern in terms of the ordinal position of the registered child, although this would have been affected to some extent by the sample bias towards younger children, and exclusion of siblings. In fact, eight out of twenty in this sample were first born children.

The keyworkers

Of the 20 keyworkers interviewed seven were male and 13 female. All were White British. The majority worked in generic children and family settings, and only three specialist child protection workers were interviewed. The social workers had a large range of levels of experience, from one year after qualifying to 27 years of professional social work. The mean number of years qualified across the sample is 11.3 years, so this represented a set of experienced practitioners.

All the social workers bar one (newly qualified) had received some child protection training, usually in the form of in house foundation training organised by the ACPC. Some had received extensive post-qualifying training in child protection social work, though only three out of twenty had any training specifically on working with neglect. Interestingly, this small amount of training on neglect was medically oriented and majored on failure to thrive.

Keyworker interviews

The interview schedule for keyworkers was piloted in a neighbouring local authority. A copy is included in the Appendix. The structured questions related to factors identified by practitioners as being significant factors in neglect. They were taken almost directly from the results of the workshop exercise described above. A few factors listed by the workshop focus groups have been amalgamated or expanded but the generic categories remain the same. There are a number of questions about the child, parents/caregivers, family dynamics, supervision, compliance and social factors. All relate to the situation at the time of registration.

The remaining questions were open ended allowing for dialogue and discussion. In this section there were 12 questions under headings: recognition, causation, working together, feelings and conclusion. Summary recording of the answers to these questions was done by the researcher during the interview.

Of the 20 keyworkers interviewed 19 were interviewed face to face but one had to be interviewed by telephone.

Case management

The majority of families in the sample were already known to Social Services. However, the keyworkers interviewed named a variety of different avenues of referral leading to registration which illustrates the fact that the recognition of neglect is an inter-agency matter. Five referrals arose directly out of ongoing involvement by Social Services, four came via the Emergency Duty Team or the Police and three from hospital social workers. The Health Services are represented by three referrals from health visitors (community) and one from a midwife (hospital). One referral came from school, one from Education Welfare and two were by direct parental request.

Comments by keyworkers about working with other agencies were overwhelmingly positive: 18 said that they felt supported by colleagues from other agencies; 17 reported that there was a functioning core group for the case they were co-ordinating; and 14 reported clear consensus about the issue of registration at case conference. These figures are relatively high given the complex nature of neglect cases and the negative feelings reported by workers in the workshop. Inter-agency communication is crucially important to the way in which register cases are managed and, with respect to the cases in the sample, the inter-agency approach would appear to be working well.

In view of the feelings reported in the workshop (which closely correspond to one of the themes running through the literature review), it is perhaps surprising that a large proportion of keyworkers (14 out of 20) expressed optimism about future outcomes. A clear majority felt that they had made a difference for the better in the life of the registered child.

It was noticeable that the level of optimism seemed to be related to the age of the child so that the earlier the intervention the more optimism the keyworker was inclined to express (this also links in with comments made by keyworkers about the importance of early intervention in neglect cases). Keyworker morale was therefore higher than might be expected given the apparently unrewarding nature of the work. A guarded optimism was the most commonly expressed feeling, as illustrated by the worker who says: 'they'll never be perfect parents, but, with support, they'll manage and the kids will survive'. Most keyworkers expressed satisfaction with the supervision they received on these cases though a minority were without a team leader which clearly made it difficult to provide regular, supportive supervision.

Significant features of neglect

When asked to assess whether the list of 'significant features' identified in the workshops were found in the case under discussion, the keyworkers responses indicated a high level of agreement with the assessment of the Focus Groups (Table 8).

The aggregate scores in Table 8 represent the frequency with which each feature was identified by the 20 keyworkers as relevant to their case. The scores cannot be interpreted simplistically in terms of a checklist of causal factors in neglect cases. There is a complex interrelationship between the different factors which would take further, more sophisticated, analysis to separate out in terms of causal relationships. They do however illustrate certain recurring themes in neglect cases. These themes have already been identified by practitioners as being important in defining neglect in an operational way in the child protection process. The scores given here to various factors may give some indication as to the sort of 'weighting' they have with respect to this sample of cases.

The structured interview schedule lists 35 different factors which workshop participants had identified as being potentially significant in neglect cases. Looking at the scores case by case the mean score for the number of different factors thought to be significant per individual case was 18.5. This means that most cases in the sample score highly in terms of the number of different factors which were thought to be significant in reaching the conclusion that the child subject has been neglected.

Table 8 Significant features of neglect - keyworkers' rankings of relevance to their chosen case

	Features identified by Focus Groups	Relevant to Keyworkers' Cases
Features concerning child	delayed development	6
	lack of stimulation	11
	behaviour problems	8
	aggression	6
	physical injury/abuse	5
	sexual abuse/ disinhibited sexuality	4
	poor hygiene	9
	hunger/feeding problems/ inadequate diet	8
	failure to thrive	3
	health problems/ inappropriate medical requests	5
Parents / Caregivers	poor parenting of caregivers	18
	history of neglect/ abuse in caregivers	16
	caregivers experienced care system/ prison	12
	substance abuse	10
	mental illness/ learning disability	11
	inability to nurture/ lack of bonding	11
	poor parenting skills	14
	disorganisation/ mismanagement	18
Family Dynamics	high stress levels	17
	family violence	13
	unrealistic expectations of child	13
	parents needs first	14
	scapegoating	4
	lack of boundaries	10
Supervision	lack of supervision	10
	inappropriate carers	7
Compliance	family known to SSD	18
	resistant/ non-cooperative	9
	failure to keep appointments	14
	poor school attendance	5
Social Factors	poverty/ deprivation	15
	debts, financial problems	18
	unemployment/ reliance on benefits	17
	poor housing	6
	social isolation	10

Base: 20 Keyworkers' Cases

This mean figure masks a considerable range of different scores ranging from six (lowest number of factors in one case) to 27 (highest number of factors in one case). The distribution of scores for multiplicity of factors is illustrated in Figure 2. It is significant that the three cases which have the lowest scores (six, eight and eight factors respectively) prove, on closer examination, to be atypical. One of these cases relates to a child whose mother is alcoholic and, apart from one isolated incident, appears to offer a satisfactory level of care to her son. The second relates to a child whose mother, in a moment of crisis, made a dramatic gesture which put the child at risk. The third concerns a child who was badly burned in a house fire whilst in the 'care' of his extended family: in this case the concerns relate primarily to the mother's family of origin (ie maternal grandparents and extended family members). The two cases which score the highest (27 factors each), by contrast, are both long term cases of chronic neglect. A cluster of factors which were identified in the highest number of cases were those familiar from the literature review. Poor parenting, parental histories of abuse, families previously known to social services; high stress levels; debts and financial problems, poverty, unemployment, and disorganisation. All were mentioned in at least three quarters of cases.

The answers were grouped along the same dimensions as those used in the focus groups. Factors relating to the child were among the least likely to be identified by keyworkers as significant features of their case. Only one, lack of stimulation featured in more than half of the sample. However, one quarter of the sample children were registered at birth or shortly thereafter. In these cases the baby had not had time to develop any of the 'symptoms' listed so that these factors are not applicable. It is rather the widespread concern about the potential risk of the baby developing such symptoms that accounts for registration. In neglect, risk of future harm is a very important dimension of concern,

Figure 2 Significant features of neglect - in keyworkers' cases

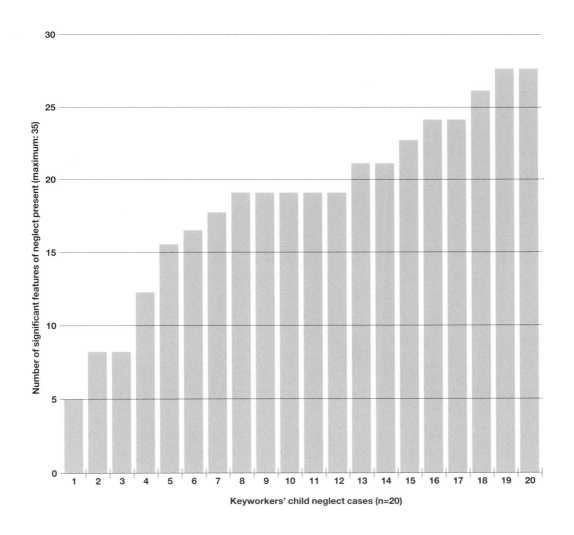

despite being very difficult to evidence. The lower scores may also be a function of the fact that assessments are not always as child-centred as ideally they should be and so some of this information may not be available. The highest scores in this section are for lack of stimulation, followed by poor hygiene, behaviour problems and issues around feeding and diet.

Factors relating to the parents/caregivers score consistently highly and seem therefore to be intrinsic to the way neglect is defined in operational terms. This is reflected in typical keyworker comments like 'Mum has never experienced effective, nurturing parenting herself' and 'Mum is preoccupied with her own unfulfilled needs'. A surprising 12 out of 20 parents/caregivers in the sample had personal experience of the care system or prison and nearly all of them (18) were regarded by keyworkers as having been poorly parented themselves. A large proportion of keyworkers indicated, by responses made to open questions about the causation of neglect, that they locate the cause of neglect in this area.

Substance abuse was a significant feature in half of the sample cases and mental illness or learning disability in 11 out of 20. The vast majority of parents (18) were seen as being disorganised and lacking in basic parenting skills. One worker commented 'this family is neglectful and chaotic in all areas of its life'.

Some of the highest scores in the sample were for the features identified as family dynamics. High stress levels were reported in 17 families in the sample and family violence in 15. One worker talked about 'appalling parental relationship leading to extreme domestic violence'. Parents putting their own needs before the needs of the child was a common theme (14), as was unrealistic expectations of the child. Scapegoating was regarded as being significant in only four sample families. Half of the sample cases were seen by keyworkers as families in which there is a lack of clarity about boundaries.

Once again, the scores for lack of supervision (10) and inappropriate carers (7) are surprisingly low. This could perhaps reflect the difficulty of actually evidencing lack of supervision, particularly with babies, or the fact that incidents of leaving alone tend to get overlooked in chaotic families. Alternatively, it could be further indication of lack of a professional consensus on the importance of supervision in assessing neglect.

Some of the factors relating to the issue of compliance were identified as significant features by a number of keyworkers. Eighteen out of 20 sample families were known to Social Services before the concerns which led to registration. This illustrates another limitation in the sort of 'snapshot picture' presented by such a survey in that the longitudinal dimension of developments over time is missing. Most of these cases are long term, sometimes with social work involvement over two generations. This long term involvement by Social Services in the life of these families means that the families concerned experience a degree of intervention which they may well see as being 'intrusive' rather than 'supportive'. Compliance, so far as they are concerned, is a loaded term.

Some of these families are seen by professionals involved as being actively resistant, but more as simply disorganised, so that failing to keep appointments is a significant factor in 14 cases. The score for poor school attendance or persistent lateness is low (five), but this is simply a function of the age range of the sample. For older children school attendance is a problem for four out of five.

Apart from housing, scores were consistently high in the section on social factors. Children registered for neglect tend to come from families suffering social and economic deprivation. Seventeen out of 20 sample families relied on state benefits to survive and 18 are described by their keyworker as having financial problems. There would appear to be an undeniable link between socio-economic hardship and neglect.

Suggestions for improving services

The social workers interviewed made a number of suggestions as to how their ACPC could improve its services to neglected children. One of the most popular suggestions was that more priority should be given to family support, early intervention and prevention. Keyworkers felt that they were in danger of becoming mere investigators and case managers and that the broader child welfare aspects of their role were overlooked because of the stress on risk and protection. Several keyworkers expressed concern about 'children in need' not getting a service at all until their situation deteriorated to crisis point, at which time they became 'children at risk' and received a child protection service.

Another suggestion, which also reflected the desire for prevention to be given greater priority, was that a family aide/family support worker could play a crucial role in families under pressure. This role could be about providing practical support and guidance in parenting and would have the further advantage of freeing social workers to do assessment and therapeutic work. There would appear to be a great deal of scope for child protection agencies to work together in providing creative and flexible 'packages of care/support' for families where children are at risk of neglect.

More training was felt to be a priority, specifically in the area of helping keyworkers to make structured assessments of neglecting families. A common perception is that, as a form of maltreatment, neglect is a difficult area to measure objectively or prove to the satisfaction of a court and that there is therefore a tendency, on the part of professionals involved, to collude in situations which are unacceptable for children.

Summary and conclusions

Ideas developed in the practitioner's workshop were collated and used to explore characteristics of a sample of 20 child neglect cases. Keyworkers were asked whether the 35 factors identified in the workshops as 'significant features' of child neglect were present in the real cases they worked with.

Results showed high levels of agreement between the keyworkers and the workshop practitioners on the importance of many features of neglect. Most notable were characteristics of the parents and family dynamics, including: poor parenting, disorganisation and lack of social skills, histories of parental abuse, high stress and illness levels and social factors such as poverty and unemployment. Most of the sample of child neglect cases showed more than half of the features identified by the workshop participants. Keyworkers also reported 'non compliance' in neglectful families and gave relatively little importance to supervision or lack of it. Unlike the workshop participants, however, keyworkers were 'cautiously optimistic' about the prospects for neglecting families and their children, and saw themselves as making a difference in the lives of the children and their families. It was not possible to know from this study whether the keyworkers were realistic, or were conforming to the 'rule of optimism'.

A number of keyworkers also described their anxiety that work with neglecting families was too concerned with investigation rather than support, an issue which has been identified in a number of recent studies of child protection services and has become the centre of a debate on the 'refocusing' of child protection (Department of Health, 1995).

5 Child neglect - a time for reappraisal

Overview of findings

In a two stage examination of practitioners' perspectives on neglect, it was shown that neglect profiles developed in discussion with practitioners had validity when applied to a sample of real cases. Practitioners' assumptions, based on their experience of working with neglecting families, were made explicit in the workshops and tested out in the survey. Results clarified a number of characteristic features of child neglect.

Firstly, neglect is a complex and multi-faceted phenomenon which is difficult to define. Out of a possible 35 different factors identified by practitioners as significant in defining neglect, the mean score for the number of factors reported as being significant per individual case was 18.5. This implies that there is no one particular factor which, taken alone, can be used to define neglect; no simple litmus test will reveal the presence or absence of neglect. It also follows that there is a great variety in the possible permutations of combinations of factors present in a particular case. The greater the number of factors taken into account, the more possible combinations of different factors are available. Because of this it would appear to be very difficult to describe a 'typical' case. This is illustrated by the fact that the only single factors which each of the sample cases, without exception, have in common are built into the sample itself: eg they are all registered and they all have a keyworker. Neglect may therefore be considered to be a loosely defined category indicative of professional concern about standards of child care. In the neglect workshop some evidence was found to suggest possible agency differences, and in some areas professional consensus was much lower than others, particularly in relation to supervision.

Secondly neglect is long term. Ninety percent of sample families were previously known to social services, many of them over a considerable length of time. These tended to be families with many problems who absorbed a great deal of professional input. It was not uncommon for levels of professional concern and involvement to ebb and flow in response to life events within the family, resulting in a sequence of registration, de-registration and re-registration. With neglect it was not usually one particular incident or one risk factor on its own which led to registration, it was the accumulation of worrying factors over time.

Because of the long term, chronic nature of the problem of child neglect the issue of compliance becomes crucial. It is not just a matter of whether deficits in the standard of child care are present within the home. These deficits may, after all, be overcome by the provision of compensatory care experiences for the children concerned (such as day care, nursery places, or respite care). However, this depends on the family co-operating with service providers. It is when the deficits in care cannot be overcome because of the family's resistance that the likelihood of the children suffering significant harm is greatest. The workshop gave clear indications that professionals view neglecting families as being non-compliant, and the survey broadly supported this view.

Of all the generic categories in Table 8, factors relating to parents/caregivers appear to be integral to the way in which neglect is defined in practice. Eighteen out of twenty cases scored positively for 'poor parenting of caregivers' and 'disorganisation/ mismanagement'. Many caregivers were thought to have a history of neglect or abuse in their own lives, and 12 out of 20 had personal experience of the care system or prison. Substance abuse and mental illness or learning disability were also common. Results suggest that most caregivers were significantly damaged and disadvantaged individuals, who were ill equipped, emotionally and practically, to care for children. The data on family structure illustrate the wide diversity of living situations experienced by these children. Less than half of the sample children (8 out of 20) live with both biological parents in a conventional family setting. Nearly as many (7 out of 20) lived in reconstituting families of various sorts, mostly consisting of mother plus a new male partner. The relationship between neglect and family structure is further complicated by the fact that families evolve and change over time so any description of family structure is a provisional and approximate one.

The results underline the importance of emotional/relationship factors in the definition of neglect. It is clear that for a child to be registered under the category of neglect there must be more at stake than the fact that the child may be receiving a low level of material care. Relationship issues and family dysfunction are central to practitioners' understandings of how children become neglected. They considered that it was not simply poverty that leads to children being neglected; rather, it was that, in situations of scarcity and pressure, children's needs are overlooked or take second place to those of adults. Social workers seem to construe neglect in terms of a deficit in care giving rather than a simple lack of resources.

It is undeniably true however that social factors connected with poverty and deprivation scored consistently highly throughout the sample. Neglected children suffered from poverty both in their material and their emotional environments. It is this combination which is so damaging for these multiply disadvantaged children and which may be responsible for much of the harm caused by neglect.

Common themes in research on neglect

Although there has been relatively little research on practitioner perspectives, the present research in many ways supports findings from the few studies which have been carried out. Minty and Pattinson (1994), in a study of families referred to an NSPCC Child Protection team, conclude that physical neglect is almost always associated with emotional neglect. Minty and Pattinson comment:

"there would appear to be validity in a global concept of neglect, in which neglect is always more than not being able to afford certain necessities for children. The families that were referred to the NSPCC, and were subsequently judged to be neglectful, were not on the whole families where there was simply material hardship." (Minty and Pattinson, 1994, p746)

As with any form of maltreatment it is the emotional context within which the maltreatment habitually occurs which is most likely to do the greatest damage to the developing personality. O'Hagan stresses the need to consider the welfare of the child in its entirety, including emotional and psychological development, throughout the child protection process (O'Hagan, 1993). In its summary of current research on child protection the Department of Health uses the concept of 'low warmth/high criticism' to refer to the emotional context within which abuse and neglect frequently occur (Department of Health, 1995).

The present results also accord with the results of research presenting a health visitor perspective on neglect (Savage, 1994). Savage conducted a comparative study of neglecting and non-neglecting families in Northern Ireland, in order to ascertain whether it is possible to observe early indicators of neglect. She found that indicators of neglect were present in the neglecting sample and concluded therefore that neglect may be assumed to be predictable. The neglecting families she looked at had a multitude of problems, the most significant, in her estimation, being lack of support: 80% reported poor relationships with partners and 65% poor extended family support. Savage's sample of neglecting families showed relatively high levels of parental disturbance (45% of mothers and 25% of fathers from 'unstable family backgrounds'). These proportions are somewhat smaller than those found here although comparisons are not straightforward because of the vague and unspecific nature of the description 'unstable family background'. She also found that alcohol abuse was a significant factor in 75% of mothers and 45% of fathers. She concluded that there was a great amount of loss present in the lives of the mothers and children of the neglecting group.

These differential findings for mothers and fathers of neglected children point to an ethical and methodological problem in research on child neglect. It has long been customary in our society to assume that mothers bear the greatest degree of responsibility for the practical and emotional nurture of their children (Milner, 1993). This is reflected in the design of research programmes and the language used by researchers who talk of the 'neglectful mother'. In reading some of the studies one cannot help wondering where the fathers are and, indeed, their absence or marginality in neglecting families may itself be a contributory factor in the genesis of neglect.

Taking parents/caregivers as a generic category (the approach which was adopted in this study) may appear to be less oppressive towards mothers in that shared responsibility is assumed. However, in the light of what actually happens in neglecting families this assumption is perhaps rather naive and runs the risk of masking important differences in gender roles and responsibilities within the home (Lacharite, Ethier and Couture, 1996).

Polansky (1985) also reports that neglectful families live in less supportive environments. In a later article study Polansky and his associates report on a longitudinal study of neglectful families in which they found that: 'the mother and children nearly always are attached to each other, but they are the only consistent unit, otherwise all is change' (Polansky, Gaudin and Kilpatrick, 1992c, p26). The intense volatility and changeability which characterises such households makes Polansky question whether these are 'families', in the conventional sense of the word, at all. The chemical analogy of the 'radical' is used to portray the sense of family fragments in changing constellations within which the mother-child bond is paramount. The findings on family structure in the research reported here support this analogy, particularly with respect to the more chaotic neglecting families.

Recommendations for further research

This is a small scale study, based in one local authority area. Furthermore, the children who are registered for neglect under the target authority's procedures may not be comparable to those children registered as being neglected in other authorities. Gibbons, Conroy and Bell, in their large scale survey of English child protection registers, documented wide variations in interpreting categories for registration and in deciding thresholds for intervention (Gibbons, Conroy and Bell, 1995). Fisher, Miller and Sinclair looked at which children are registered at case conference and found that operational factors accounted for large variations both within and between local authorities (Fisher, Miller and Sinclair, 1995).

The findings of the present study relate to children who are registered for neglect rather than the neglected child per se. It is widely recognised that there is a significant difference between the prevalence of maltreatment in society and its incidence as reflected in official child protection statistics. Registers are kept for policy and organisational reasons and are, at best, only an approximate guide as to what may pertain in the undocumented, secret lives of children. Campbell compared children on the register with other children who were not registered and found that there were few significant differences between the two groups (Campbell, 1991). Little and Gibbons (1993) attempted to predict rates of registration using complicated calculations to take account of social and demographic factors. The index they devised had a predictive reliability of only 60% and they concluded:

"the children who end up on the register are only a small minority of all ill-treated children… We must not therefore treat register statistics as valid measures of child abuse and neglect." (Little and Gibbons, 1993, p18)

Furthermore, registration is just one point in the official child protection process. The Department of Health uses the concept of 'thresholds of intervention' in its discussion of the child protection process (Department of Health, 1995). The research summarised in 'Messages from Research' demonstrates that at each threshold (from initial allegation, to enquiry, to case conference, to registration) a proportion of cases drop out of the system. This filtering process means that the cases which eventually get registered represent a small proportion of the total number of families about whom there are official concerns.

Consequently, the findings of the present study are not necessarily generalisable to the large number of cases of neglect which are the subject of professional concern but which are not registered, although some previous research indicates that there may be few, if any, differences between registered and unregistered children.

One methodological limitation inherent in the sample survey is that it lacks a longitudinal dimension. The survey gives a snapshot 'still life' of the situation pertaining at the particular moment of time when the survey is being conducted. Because neglect is a long term chronic problem rather than an acute crisis, and as the situation of children in neglecting families is often very volatile, this is a significant limitation.

The strengths of this research lie in its use of a mix of different methods, giving the findings a comprehensiveness and depth they might otherwise lack. The results give some clear indications as to what serious neglect looks like as seen through the eyes of practitioners. A number of significant themes emerge from the sample of neglect cases surveyed and these are described in the words of the child protection workers whose perceptions of neglect are the subject of this study.

The field of child neglect is under-researched both in social work and in related disciplines. Most British research has been small scale and exploratory in nature; there is nothing which approaches the scale, or the scientific rigour, of Polansky's work in America. Of the 20 research studies summarised and evaluated in the recent Department of Health publication 'Messages from Research' (Department of Health, 1995), over half are concerned with sexual abuse. Three major research projects focus on physical abuse but neglect has been virtually ignored. Even the research which is more generic in nature pays little attention to issues of child neglect.

In terms of the identification and assessment of neglect there is a pressing need for further clarification of the differences between neglecting and non-neglecting families. This research has attempted to identify some of the major significant features common to neglecting families but further studies are required. In particular some controlled studies comparing neglecting and non-neglecting families would generate useful data for further analysis.

A major national prevalence study of neglect would be a significant advance. Practitioners express the opinion that child neglect is common and pervasive, yet there is little in the way of hard evidence to back up this impression. Wynne for example concludes:

"neglect is insidious, pervasive and the commonest yet least recognised form of child maltreatment." (Hobbs, Hanks and Wynne, 1993)

If this contention is true a prevalence study would provide invaluable evidence that the priorities of our current child protection system need rethinking.

A less ambitious project would be to analyse national register statistics with particular reference to neglect. Although register statistics are notoriously unreliable as a guide to the actual incidence of child maltreatment they do give some indication as to the minimum scale of the problem. The most recent statistics available from the Department of Health (Department of Health, 1995) show that neglect accounts for roughly 25% of children on child protection registers nationally, increasing to 30% if mixed categories are included. In his discussion of neglect registrations Parton states:

"in many respects it is the fastest growing category and is now bigger than sexual abuse"
(Parton, 1995, p68)

A number of studies have demonstrated that there is a high degree of 'crossover' between different types of maltreatment (Farmer and Owen, 1995) and some research designed to clarify the commonalities and distinctives as between different categories of maltreatment might generate some very interesting data. There seems to be a particularly strong link between physical abuse and physical neglect and between emotional abuse and passive neglect. In fact one has to question whether such distinctions are meaningful conceptually or helpful in terms of practical interventions. Such a study might point the way towards a different, more sensitive, way of conceptualising and measuring significant harm which would do more justice to the complexity of children's developmental needs.

The results of this research once again underline the strong association between poverty, deprivation and neglect. Yet this relationship is complex and poorly understood. It cannot be assumed that poor families neglect their children or that neglected children are necessarily poor. One could speculate that emotional neglect might also occur among higher income groups when parents are so busy pursuing their careers that their children's needs for time, attention and affirmation take second place. Further research, utilising a broad sociological perspective, on the relationship between poverty, health issues and neglect could provide invaluable evidence for policy makers and planners.

A perspective which is missing from the research reported here is that of the victims. Professionals who work with neglecting families need to have some awareness of what it feels like to be a victim of neglect. A retrospective study involving interviews of survivors could provide invaluable information about the impact of neglect on child victims. Such information would have implications both for working in partnership with neglecting families and therapeutic work with survivors.

One theoretical approach which shows a great deal of promise in terms of the causation of neglect is attachment theory. Although there is a growing body of research evidence showing strong associations between attachment difficulties and child maltreatment generally (see Chapter Two), there is little which specifically links neglect to dysfunctional parent-child relationships. Research which compared parent-child attachments in neglecting and non-neglecting families could provide powerful explanatory concepts for practitioners. Attachment theory could also provide a useful practice orientation for therapeutic work with neglecting families.

Implications for practice

The professional confusion which is documented in the present research indicates the need for training for child protection workers specifically around neglect. This has also been emphasised in the Bridge Child Care Consultancy Service's recent report, 'Paul: Death Through Neglect' (Bridge Child Care Consultancy Service, 1995). Whilst no amount of training can take away the complexities and ambiguities inherent in this type of work, high quality training can give workers greater confidence in making professional judgements so that they are less likely to react in a way which is either oppressive towards families or professionally dangerous.

Some evidence is emerging that social workers tend to underestimate the importance of neglect (Minty and Pattinson, 1994; Tomison, 1995; Stevenson, 1996). There is a 'common-sense' assumption that neglect does not really matter and that its consequences for children are unlikely to be very damaging (Moore, 1994). Fitzgerald argues that this is untrue and concludes:

"we hope that the demonstration of the existence of neglect not solely related to poverty, as we have established throughout the report, removes the myth that children do not die of neglect in 1994."
(Bridge Child Care Consultancy Service, 1995, p201)

It follows that the recognition of neglect is an important issue for the child protection community and the present research strongly supports the recommendation contained in the inquiry on 'Pauls' death.

"we recommend that the Department of Health, Department of Education and Science, the Home Office and the Welsh Office review its guidelines to agencies working in the child protection field with a view to providing more detailed practice guidance concerning the identification of neglect and its effect upon children. Guidance should include ways in which instances of neglect can be quantified."
(Bridge Child Care Consultancy Service, 1995, p179)

The multi-factorial nature of neglect described in the research reported here makes the task of the assessment of neglect more challenging and difficult. Assessments which take account of the multiplicity of factors which may be present in neglecting families will need to be truly comprehensive and multi-disciplinary. Regular high quality information on the physical development of the child (the health visitor's role is crucial here) is essential, together with information relating to the child's emotional state and the quality of parent-child interactions. The keyworker who co-ordinates the assessment needs to look at the welfare of the child in a holistic way which is less concerned with incidents and events and more concerned with context and process.

The analysis of feelings produced by working with neglect, has important implications in terms of supervision. For those who manage front line workers the question 'who cares for the carers?' is unavoidable and constitutes one of the major challenges facing service providers. Regular, supportive and disciplined supervision of staff is clearly essential. Such supervision, if it is to do justice to the emotional reactions produced by close contact with distressing and confusing situations, will need to be about more than simple accountability and assessing whether agency procedures have been followed or not. In more complex and demanding cases outside consultation, independent of agency line management, may be required.

Partnership with parents is a major theme in the Children Act and the attempt to implement this principle is transforming child protection practice. The data gathered in this research on compliance indicates that partnership is a crucial, if problematic, issue in working with neglecting families. Child protection professionals reported that they viewed neglecting families as being non-compliant and uncooperative. In terms of partnership practice this is not encouraging. Core group members need a model of partnership practice which actually works long term in the complex, often chaotic, world of neglecting families. They need an approach to intervening in these families which empowers parents/caregivers as well as protecting children. The marginal role of male partners in many neglecting families presents a strong challenge to social workers and others to find new ways of engaging and working constructively with men.

Services for children in need has also emerged as a major theme for child welfare agencies to consider in the current 'refocusing' debate, following the publication of 'Child Protection: Messages from Research', (Department of Health, 1995). There is a widespread feeling that too many children are being treated as 'children at risk' whereas 'children in need' are being relatively neglected. The implications in terms of neglect are that a proportion of the less seriously neglected children who are currently being dealt with under child protection procedures might, more appropriately, be dealt with under Section 17 of the Children Act (ie as children in need).

However, this is not a simple matter as 'children in need' and 'children at risk' are not discrete, separate groups. It is important therefore that Local Authorities devise strategies for children in need which are related to their child protection procedures in such a way that a child may move from the 'children in need route' to the 'child protection route' and vice versa. For example, one of the major criticisms of the way that Paul and his family were dealt with in Islington was that agencies responded to Paul as a 'child in need' with practical support and financial help whilst tragically overlooking the question of whether he was safe ((Bridge Child Care Consultancy Service, 1995). The delicate balance between intrusive over reaction on the one hand and complacent under reaction on the other still proves illusive. At the level of public policy it seems likely that there will always be a degree of tension between prevention and protection and the relative priority accorded to each will vary with local circumstances and current thinking.

The debate about children in need is part of a wider debate about social policy. Over the past 20 years there has been a steady shift from universal to more selective forms of welfare provision. This has been paralleled by a shift in thinking within the child care professions from a broad child welfare approach to a narrower child protection focus. Parton is one prominent social commentator who regrets this shift. He believes that it has had a detrimental effect on the lives of children and families. His assessment is that:

"to have the best chance of preventing the more serious family and child care problems, what we might call child neglect, the best chance of success is to improve and develop universal, non-stigmatising services which are integrated into the mainstream of social provision for children" (Parton, 1995, pp75-76)

One area of public policy which would have an incontrovertible impact on child neglect would be a radical and comprehensive anti-poverty strategy. The links between poverty and child neglect are well documented and show up clearly in this study. Unfortunately for children all the indications are that child poverty is on the increase. In this respect it is our social policy which is neglectful in allowing conditions to develop in which children suffer unnecessary harm due to material deprivation (Segal and Gustavsson, 1990). The neglect of children is an indictment not just of those families which fail to meet the basic needs of their children but also of a society which fails to construct and maintain an infrastructure which facilitates parenting and values children.

Finally, and most importantly, there is the question of child protection priorities. The conclusion of Nelson and her colleagues, though it refers to the American context, has powerful resonances with the current child protection scene in the UK:

"Given the potentially lethal consequences of neglect and its recurrent nature that makes it so destructive to families and children over time, child neglect cases must receive a greater priority in systems that now deal almost exclusively with child physical and sexual abuse. Anything less than unswerving commitment to new policy and practice initiatives for families suffering from child neglect represents an abrogation of social work's responsibility to its most vulnerable clients." (Nelson, Saunders and Landsman, 1993, p670)

The profile of child neglect urgently needs to be raised both on the public and on the professional child protection agendas. For too long our attitude towards neglected children has been one of indifference. The neglect of children by their caregivers is mirrored in the attitude of official child welfare agencies. We have bought into the lie that these children's lives are not worth bothering about. It is a sad reflection on our national child protection strategy (or lack of it) that it has taken yet another tragic child death to jolt the system into activity and to initiate a debate about the harmful consequences of neglect.

References

Adcock, A. and White, R. (Eds) (1985). **Good Enough Parenting: A Framework for Assessment.** BAAF Practice Series No.12.

Ainsworth, M.D. (1969). Object relations, dependency and attachment: a theoretical review of the infant–mother relationship. *Child Development, 40,* 969–1025.

Allen, C.M. and Epperson, D.L. (1993). Perpetrator gender and type of child maltreatment: overcoming limited conceptualisations and obtaining representative samples. *Child Welfare, (72)6,* 543–554.

Allen, R.E. and Oliver, J.M. (1982). The effects of child maltreatment on language development. *Child Abuse and Neglect, (6),* 299–305.

Alter, C.F. (1985). Decision making factors in cases of child neglect. *Child Welfare, (64)2,* 99–111.

Ammerman, R.T. (1990). Etiological models of child maltreatment: a behavioral perspective. *Behavior Modification, (14)3,* 230–254.

Ards, S. and Harrell, A. (1993). Reporting of child maltreatment: a secondary analysis of the national incidence surveys. *Child Abuse and Neglect, 17,* 339–344.

Baldwin, N. and Spencer, N. (1993). Deprivation and child abuse: implications for strategic planning. *Children and Society, (7)4,* 357–375.

Batchelor, J. (1990). **Failure to Find Failure to Thrive: The Case for Improving Screening, Prevention and Treatment in Primary Care.** London: Whiting and Birch.

Belsky, J. (1993). Etiology of child maltreatment: a developmental ecological analysis. *Psychological Bulletin, (114)3,* 413–434.

Berkowitz, C.D., Logan, M.K. and Sklaren, B.C. (1985). Striving for thriving. *Protecting Children, 2,* 19–22.

Besharov, D.J. (1981). Towards better research on child abuse and neglect: making definitional issues an explicit methodological concern. *Child Abuse and Neglect, 5,* 383–390.

Besharov, D.J. (1985). Doing something about child abuse: the need to narrow the grounds for state intervention. *Harvard Journal of Law and Public Policy, 8,* 539–589.

Bolton, F.G. (1983). **When Bonding Fails: Clinical Assessments of High-Risk Families.** Newbury Park: Sage Publications.

Boushel, M. (1994). The protective environment of children: towards a framework for anti-oppressive, cross-cultural and cross-national understanding. *British Journal of Social Work, 24,* 173–190.

Bradshaw, J. (1990). **Child Poverty and Deprivation in the United Kingdom.** London: National Children's Bureau.

Brayden, R.M., Altemeier, W.A., Tucker, D.D., Dietrich, M.S. and Vietze, P. (1992). Antecedents of child neglect in the first two years. *Paediatrics, (120)3,* 426–429.

Bridge Child Care Consultancy Service. (1995). **Paul: Death Through Neglect.**
London: Bridge Care Consultancy Service on behalf of Islington ACPC.

Bronfenbrenner, U. (1977). Toward an experimental ecology of human development.
American Psychologist, July, 513-531.

Brown, G.W. and Harris, T.O. (1978). **Social Origins of Depressions.** London:
Tavistock.

Calam, R. and Franchi, C. (1987). **Child Abuse and its Consequences:
Observational Approaches.** Cambridge: Cambridge University Press.

Campbell, M. (1991). Children at risk: how different are children on the child protection
register? *British Journal of Social Work, 21,* 259-275.

Cann, A.J. (1989). The indefinition of child abuse. *Child Abuse Review, 3(2),* 27-29.

Channer, Y. and Parton, N. (1990). Racism, cultural relativism and child protection.
Pages 105-120 in **Treating Child Abuse Seriously** by the Violence Against Children
Study Group. London: Unwin/Hyman.

Christensen, M.J., Brayden, R.M., Dietrich, M.S., Mclaughlin, F.J., Sherrod, K.B. and
Altemeier, W.A. (1994). The prospective assessment of self-concept in neglectful and
physically abusive low income mothers. *Child Abuse and Neglect, (18)3,* 225-232.

Christopherson, J. (1993). The Children Act 1989 and Child Protection 1993. In L.
Waterhouse (Ed) **Child Abuse and Child Abusers.** London: Jessica Kingsley.

Clausen, A.H. and Crittenden, P.M. (1991). Physical and psychological maltreatment:
relations among types of child maltreatment. *Child Abuse and Neglect, 15,* 5-18.

Cleaver, H. and Freeman, P. (1995). **Parental Perspectives in Cases of Suspected
Child Abuse.** London: HMSO.

Codega, J. (1989). Treatment of the neglectful parent. *Protecting Children, (6)3,* 8-12.

Corby, B. (1993). **Child Abuse, Towards a Knowledge Base.**
Oxford: Oxford University Press.

Corby, B. and Mills, C. (1986). Child abuse: risks and resources. *British Journal of Social
Work, 16,* 531-542.

Cooper, A. (1995). Britain in a moral panic. Part 4: silence that cloaked child sex conspiracy. *Community Care, 3-9 August,* i-viii.

Cooper, D.M. (1993). **Child Abuse Revisited.** Buckingham: Open University Press.

Covitz, J. (1986). **Emotional Child Abuse: The Family Curse.** Boston: Sigo Press.

Craft, J.L. and Staudt, M. (1991). Reporting and founding of child neglect in urban and
rural communities. *Child Welfare, (70)3,* 359-370.

Creighton, S.J. and Russell, N. (1995). **Voices from Childhood: A Survey of
Childhood Experiences and Attitudes to Child Rearing Among Adults in the
United Kingdom.** London: NSPCC.

Crittenden, P.M. (1988). Distorted patterns of relationship in maltreating families: the
role of internal representation model. *Journal of Reproductive and Infant Psychology, 6,* 183-
199.

Crittenden, P.M. (1993). An information-processing perspective on the behaviour of
neglectful parents. *Criminal Justice and Behaviour, (20)1,* 27-48.

Crouch, J. L. and Milner, J.S. (1993). Effects of child neglect on children. *Criminal Justice and Behaviour, (20)1,* 49-65.

Daro, D. (1988). **Confronting Child Abuse: Research for Effective Programme Design.** New York: Free Press.

Daws, D. (1994). Family relationships and infant feeding problems. *Health Visitor, (67)5,* 162-164.

Department of Health. (1988). **Protecting Children: A Guide for Social Workers Undertaking a Comprehensive Assessment.** London: HMSO.

Department of Health. (1991). **Child Abuse: A Study of Inquiry Reports 1980-1989.** London: HMSO.

Department of Health. (1995). **Child Protection: Messages from Research.** London: HMSO.

Department of Health. (1996). **Children and Young People on Child Protection Registers: Year Ending 31 March 1995.** London: Government Statistical Service.

Department of Health and Social Security. (1980). **Child Abuse: Central Register Systems,** LASSL(80)4. HN(80)20.

Department of Health and Social Security. (1982). **Child Abuse: A Study of Inquiry Reports 1973-1981.** London: HMSO.

Department of Health and Social Security and Welsh Office. (1988). **Working Together: A Guide to Arrangements for Interagency Co-operation for the Protection of Children from Abuse.** London: HMSO.

Dileonardi, J.W. (1993). Families in poverty and chronic neglect of children. *Families in Society, (74)9,* 557-562.

Dingwall, R. (1989). Some problems about predicting child abuse and neglect. Pages 34-53 in **Child Abuse: Public Policy and Professional Practice.** (Ed) Stevenson, O. Hemel Hempstead: Harvester Wheatsheaf.

Dingwall, R. (1992). Labelling children as abused or neglected. Pages 158-164 in *Child Abuse and Neglect.* (Eds) Stainton-Rogers, W., Henvey, D., Roche, J. and Ash, E. London: Batsford.

Dubowitz, H., Black, M., Starr, R.H. and Zuravin, S.A. (1993). A conceptual definition of child neglect. *Criminal Justice and Behaviour, (20)1,* 8-26.

Dubowitz, H., Zuckerman, D.M., Bithony, W.G. and Newberger, E.H. (1989). Child abuse and failure to thrive: individual, familial and environmental characteristics. *Violence and Victims, (4)3,* 191-201.

Dukes, R.L. and Kean, R.B. (1989). An experimental study of gender and situation in the perception and reportage of child abuse. *Child Abuse and Neglect, 13,* 351-360.

Eckenrode, J., Laird, M. and Doris, J. (1993). School performance and disciplinary problems among abused and neglected children. *Developmental Psychology, (29)1,* 53-62.

Edmundson, S.E. and Collier, P. (1993). Child protection and emotional abuse: definition, identification and usefulness within educational settings. *Educational Psychology and Practice, (8)4,* 198-206.

Egeland, B. and Erikson, M.F. (1987). Psychologically unavailable caregiving. Pages 110-120 in **Psychological Maltreatment of Children and Youth.** (Eds) Brassard, M., Germain, R. and Hart, S. New York: Pergamon.

Ethier, C.S., Lacharite, C. and Couture, G. (1995). Childhood adversity, parental stress and depression of negligent mothers. *Child Abuse and Neglect (19)5,* 619-632.

Etzioni, A. (1993). **The Parenting Deficit.** London: Demos.

Farmer, E. (1993). The impact of child protection interventions: the experiences of parents and children. In L. Waterhouse (Ed) **Child Abuse and Child Abusers.** London: Jessica Kingsley.

Farmer, E. and Owen, M. (1995). **Child Protection Practice: Private Risks and Public Remedies.** London: HMSO.

Fisher, T., Miller, L.B. and Sinclair, I. (1995). Which children are registered at case conferences? *British Journal of Social Work, (25)2,* 191-207.

Fox, S. and Dingwall, R. (1985). An exploratory study of variation in social workers' and health visitors' definitions of maltreatment. *British Journal of Social Work, 15,* 467-477.

Fraiberg, S., Adelson, E. and Shapiro, V. (1975). Ghosts in the nursery. A psycho-analytic approach to the problem of impaired infant-mother relationships. *Journal of American Academy of Child Psychiatry, 14,* 387-421.

Francis, J. (1994). Under pressure. *Community Care, 1001, 24 March 1994,* 10.

Frost, N. and Stein, M. (1989). **The Politics of Child Welfare: Inequality, Power and Change.** New York: Harvester Wheatsheaf.

Furley, A. (1989). **Bad Start in Life.** London: Shelter.

Garbarino, J.A., Guttman, E. and Seeley, J.W. (1986). **The Psychologically Battered Child.** San Francisco: Jossey-Bass Inc.

Gaudin, J.M. (1993). **Child Neglect: A Guide for Intervention.** Washington: National Center on Child Abuse and Neglect.

Gaudin, J.M., Polansky, N.A. and Kilpatrick, A.C. (1992). The child well-being scales: a field trial. *Child Welfare, (71)4,* 319-328.

Gaudin, J.M., Polansky, N.A., Kilpatrick, A.C. and Shilton, P. (1996). Family functioning in neglectful families. *Child Abuse and Neglect, (20)4,* 363-371.

Gibbons, J., Conroy, S. and Bell, C. (1995). **Operating the Child Protection Register.** London: HMSO.

Giovannoni, J.M. and Becerra, R.M. (1979). **Defining Child Abuse.** New York: The Free Press.

Giovannoni, J.M. and Billingsley, A. (1970). Child neglect among the poor: a study of parental adequacy in families of three ethnic groups. *Child Welfare, (49)4,* 196-204.

Glachan, M. (1991). Child abuse: a social and cultural phenomenon. *Early Child Development and Care, 74,* 95-102.

Hallett, C. (1993). Working together in child protection. In L. Waterhouse (Ed) **Child Abuse and Child Abusers.** London: Jessica Kingsley.

Hanks, H., Hobbs, C.J., Seymour, D. and Stratton, P. (1988). Infants who fail to thrive: an intervention for poor feeding practices. *Journal of Reproductive and Infant Psychology, 6,* 101-111.

Hartley, R. (1989). A programme blueprint for neglectful families. *Protecting Children, (6)3,* 3-7.

Hegar, R.L. and Yungman, J. (1989). Towards a causal typology of child neglect. *Children and Youth Services Review, 11,* 203-220.

Helfer, R.E. (1990). The neglect of our children. *The Pediatric Clinics of America, (37)4,* 923-942.

Helfer, R.E. (1991). Child abuse and neglect: assessment, treatment and prevention 2007. *Child Abuse and Neglect, 15(1),* 5-15.

Hewlett, S.A. (1993). **Child Neglect in Rich Nations.** New York: UNICEF.

Hobbs, C.J., Hanks, H. and Wynne, J.M. (1993). **Child Abuse and Neglect – A Clinician's Handbook.** Edinburgh: Churchill Livingstone.

Holman, B. (1994). Research review: children and poverty. *Children and Society, (8)1,* 69-72.

Home Office, Department of Health, Department of Education and Science and Welsh Office (1991). **Working Together under the Children Act 1989: A Guide to Arrangements for Inter-Agency Co-operation for the Protection of Children from Abuse.** London: HMSO.

Hutchinson, G.D. (1990). Child maltreatment: can it be defined? *Social Services Review, (64)1,* 60-78.

Iwaniec, D. (1995). **The Emotionally Abused and Neglected Child.** Chichester: John Wiley.

Iwaniec, D., Herbert, M. and Mcneish, B.S. (1985a). Social work with failure to thrive children and their families: part 1 psycho-social factors. *British Journal of Social Work, 15,* 243-259.

Iwaniec, D., Herbert, M. and Mcneish, B.S. (1985b). Social work with failure to thrive children and their families: part 2 behavioural social work intervention. *British Journal of Social Work, 15,* 375-389.

Jenner, S. (1992). The assessment and treatment of parenting skills and deficits within the framework of child protection. *ACPP Review and Newsletter, (14)5,* 288-233.

Jones, E.D. and McCurdy, K. (1992). The links between types of maltreatment and demographic characteristics of children. *Child Abuse and Neglect, (16)2,* 201-215.

Kellmer Pringle, M. (1975). **The Needs of Children: A Personal Perspective.** London: Hutchinson.

Kempe, C., Silverman, F.N., Steele, B.F. Droegemueller, W. and Silver, H.K. (1962). The battered child syndrome. *Journal of the American Medical Association, 181,* 17-24.

Kitzinger, J. (1994). The methodology of focus groups: the importance of interaction between group participants. *Sociology of Health and Illness, (16)1,* 103-121.

Knowles, C. and Mercer, S. (1992). Feminism and anti-racism: an exploration of the political possibilities. In J. Donald and A. Rattansi (Eds) **Race Culture and Difference.** Newbury Park: Sage Publications.

Korbin, J.E. (1981). **Child Abuse and Neglect: Cross-Cultural Perspectives.** California: Berkeley University of California Press.

Korbin, J.E. (1993). Cultural diversity and child maltreatment. *Violence Update, July,* 3,8-9.

Kumar, V. (1993). **Poverty and Inequality in the UK. The Effects on Children.** London: National Children's Bureau.

Kurtz, P.D., Gaudin, J.M., Wodarski, J.S. and Howing, P.T. (1993). Maltreatment and the school-aged child: school performance consequences. *Child Abuse and Neglect, (17)5,* 581-589.

Lacharite, C., Ethier, L. and Couture, G. (1996). The influence of partners on parental stress of neglectful mothers. *Child Abuse Review, (15)1,* 18-33.

Lally, J.R. (1984). Three views of child neglect: expanding visions of preventive interventions. *Child Abuse and Neglect, 8,* 243-254.

Leach, P. (1994). **Children First.** London: Michael Joseph.

Little, M. and Gibbons, J. (1993). Predicting the rate of children on the child protection register. *Research, Policy and Planning, (10)2,* 15-18.

Lindsey, D. and Kirk, S.A. (1992). The continuing crisis in social work research. *Journal of Social Work Education, (28)3.*

Loney, M. (1989). Child abuse in a social context. In W. Stainton-Rogers, D. Henvey, and E. Ash (Eds) **Child Abuse and Neglect.** Buckingham: Open University Press.

Lyon, C. (1989). Legal developments following the Cleveland Report in England – a consideration of some aspects of the Children Bill. *Journal of Social Welfare Law, 4,* 200-206.

Margolin, L. (1990). Fatal child neglect. *Child Welfare, (69)4,* 309-319.

Maslow, A. (1943). **Motivation and Personality.** New York: Harper.

McCurdy, K. and Daro, D. (1993). **Current Trends in Child Abuse Reporting and Fatalities: The Results of the 1992 Annual Fifty State Survey.** National Center on Child Abuse Research, Working Paper No 808. Chicago: NCPCA.

Melhuish, E.C. (1993). A measure of love? An overview of the assessment of attachment. *ACPC Review and Newsletter,(15)6,* 296-275.

Miller, L.B., Fisher, T. and Sinclair, I. (1993). Decisions to register children as at risk of abuse. *Social Work and Social Sciences Review, (4)2,* 101-118.

Milner, J.A. (1993). A disappearing act: the differing career paths of fathers and mothers in child protection investigations. *Critical Social Policy, 2,* 48-63.

Milner, J.S. and Robertson, K.R. (1990). Comparisons of physical child abusers, intrafamilial child sex abusers and child neglecters. *Journal of Interpersonal Violence, (5)1,* 37-48.

Minty, B. and Pattinson, G. (1994). The nature of child neglect. *British Journal of Social Work, 24,* 733-747.

Moore, J. (1989). Turning our backs on neglect. *Community Care, Part 778,4 August,* 11-12.

Moore, J. (1994). Lethal weapon. *Community Care, Part, 1011, 7 April,* 20.

Morgan, D.L. (Ed) (1993). **Successful Focus Groups.** Newbury Park: Sage Publications.

Murphy-Berman, V.A. (1994). Conceptual framework for thinking about risk assessment and case management in child protective service. *Child Abuse and Neglect, (18)2,* 193-201.

Nelson, K.E., Saunders, E.J. and Landsman, M.J. (1993). Chronic child neglect in perspective. *Social Work, (38)6,* 661–671.

Newson, J. and Newson, E. (1970). **Four Years Old in an Urban Community.** Middlesex: Pelican.

Newson, J. and Newson, E. (1978). **Seven Years Old in an Urban Community.** Middlesex: Pelican.

Nix, L.M., Pasteur, A.B. and Servance, M.A. (1988). A focus group study of sexually active black male teenagers. *Adolescence, 23, Fall,* 741–751.

Noyes, P. (1988). The unthinking cruelty. *Child International, (1)1,* 30–31,42.

O'Hagan, K. (1993). **Emotional and Psychological Abuse of Children.** Buckingham: Open University Press.

Oppenheim, C. (1993). **Poverty: The Facts.** London: CPAG.

Packman, J. and Randall, J. (1989). Decision-making at the gateway to care. Pages 54–73 in **Child Abuse: Public Policy and Professional Practice.** (Ed) Stevenson, O. Hemel Hempstead: Harvester Wheatsheaf.

Parton, N. (1979). The natural history of child abuse: a study in social problem definition. *British Journal of Social Work, 9,* 431–451.

Parton, N. (1985). **The Politics of Child Abuse.** Basingstoke: Macmillan.

Parton, N. (1986). The Beckford Report: a critical appraisal. *British Journal of Social Work, 16,* 511–530.

Parton, N. (1990). Taking child abuse seriously in **Taking Child Abuse Seriously** by the Violence against Children Study Group, 7-24. London: Unwin/Hyman.

Parton, N. (1994). The contemporary state of child protection policy and practice. Unpublished paper given at the 'Remember Maria' Conference, 29th March 1994. London: NSPCC.

Parton, N. (1995). Neglect as child protection: the political context and the practical outcomes. *Children and Society, (9)1,* 67–89.

Parton, N. and Parton, C. (1989). Child protection, the law and dangerousness. In O. Stevenson (Ed) **Child Abuse: Public Policy and Professional Practice.** Hemel Hempstead: Harvester Wheatsheaf.

Pelton, L.H. (1981). Child abuse and neglect: the myth of classlessness. In L. H. Pelton (Ed) **The Social Context of Child Abuse and Neglect.** New York: Human Sciences Press.

Pelton, L.H. (1991). Poverty and child protection. *Protecting Children, 7(4),* 3–5.

Pfohl, S.J. (1977). The discovery of child abuse. *Social Problems, 24,* 310–323.

Pitcairn, T., Waterhouse, L., Mcghee, J., Secker, J. and Sullivan, C. (1993). Evaluating parenting in child physical abuse. In L. Waterhouse (Ed) **Child Abuse and Child Abusers.** London: Jessica Kingsley.

Polansky, N.A. (1985). The psychological effect of the neglectful mother. *Child Abuse and Neglect, 9,* 265–275.

Polansky, N.A., Chalmers, M.A., Buttenwieser, E. and Williams, D.P.(1981). **Damaged Parents: An Anatomy of Child Neglect.** Chicago: University of Chicago Press.

Polansky, N.A., Gaudin, J.M. and Kilpatrick, A.C. (1992a). The child well-being scales: a field trial. *Child Welfare, (71)4*, 319-328.

Polansky, N.A., Gaudin, J.M. and Kilpatrick, A.C. (1992b). The maternal characteristics scale: a cross validation. *Child Welfare, (71)3*, 271-280.

Polansky, N.A., Gaudin, J.M. and Kilpatrick, A.C. (1992c). Family radicals. *Children and Youth Services Review, (14)1/2*, 19-26.

Reder, P., Duncan, S. and Gray, M. (1993). A new look at child abuse tragedies. *Child Abuse Review, (2)2*, 89-100.

Reid, W.J. and Smith, A.D. (1981). **Research in Social Work.** New York: Columbia University Press.

Report of an independent inquiry Commission by the County Councils and Area Health Authorities of Berkshire and Hampshire (into the circumstances surrounding Lester Chapman's death). (1979). **Lester Chapman Inquiry Report.** Reading: Berkshire County Council.

Ringwalt, C. and Caye, J. (1989). The effect of demographic factors on perception of child neglect. *Children and Youth Services Review, 11*, 133-144.

Rohner, R.P. (1986). **The Warmth Dimension: Foundations of Parental Acceptance/Rejection Theory.** Newbury Park: Sage Publications.

Rose, S.J. and Meezan, W. (1993). Defining child neglect: evolution, influences and issues. *Social Services Review, (67)2*, 279-293.

Rose, S.J. and Meezan, W. (1996). Variations in perceptions of child neglect. *Child Welfare, (75)2*, 139-160.

Rosenberg, D. and Cantwell, H. (1993). The consequences of neglect - individual and societal. *Balliere's Clinical Paediatrics, (1)1, chapter 10*, 185-210.

Sassower, R. and Grodin, M.A. (1990). A conceptual approach to child maltreatment. *Paediatrician, 17*, 74-78.

Saunders, E.J., Nelson, K. and Landsman, M.J. (1993). Racial inequality and child neglect: findings in a metropolitan area. *Child Welfare, (72)4*, 341-354.

Savage, M.J. (1994). Can early indicators of neglecting families be observed?: a comparative study of neglecting and non-neglecting families. *Child Care in Practice, (1)1*, 27-38.

Sedlak, A. (1993). Risk factors for child abuse and neglect in the US. Paper presented to the 4th European Conference on Child Abuse and Neglect. Padua, Italy March 1993.

Segal, E.A. and Gustavsson, N.S. (1990). The high cost of neglecting children: the need for a preventive policy agenda. *Child and Adolescent Social Work Journal, (7)6*, 475-485.

Seligman, M.G.P. (1972). Learned helplessness. *Annual Review of Medicine, 23*, 407-412.

Srivastava, O.P. and Polnay, L. (1997). Field trial of graded care profile (GCP) scale: a new measure of care. *Archives of Disease in Childhood, 76*, 337-340.

Skuse, D.H. (1992). Failure to thrive: current perspectives. *Current Paediatrics, 2*, 105-110.

Stainton-Rogers, W. and Stainton-Rogers, R. (1989). Taking the child abuse debate apart. In W. Stainton-Rogers, D. Henvey, and E. Ash (Eds) **Child Abuse and Neglect.** Buckingham: Open University Press.

Stein, T. and Rzepnicki, T.L. (1983). **Decision Making at Child Welfare Intake: A Handbook for Practitioners.** New York: Child Welfare League of America.

Stevenson. O. (1994). Child welfare or child protection, where are we now? Unpublished paper given at the 'Remember Maria' Conference, 29th March 1994. London: NSPCC.

Stevenson, O. (1996). Emotional abuse and neglect: a time for reappraisal. *Children and Family Social Work, (1)1,* 13-18.

Thanki, V. (1994). Ethnic diversity and child protection. *Children and Society, (8)3,* 232-244.

Thorpe, D. (1994). **Evaluating Child Protection.** Buckingham: Open University Press.

Tomison, A.M. (1995). Spotlight on child neglect. *Issues in Child Abuse Prevention, Winter 4,* 1-11.

Tonge, W.L., James, D.S. and Hillam, S.M. (1975). **Families Without Hope: A Controlled Study of 33 Problem Families.** Ashford Kent: Headly Bros for Royal College of Psychiatrists.

Tracy, E.M., Green, R.K. and Bremseth, M.D. (1993). Meeting the environmental needs of abused and neglected children: implications from a statewide survey of supportive services. *Social Work Research and Abstracts, (29)2,* 21-26.

Trube-Becker, E. (1976). **The Death of Children Following Negligence.** Paper presented to the International Congress on Child Abuse and Neglect at Geneva, Switzerland.

Tzeng, O.C.S., Jackson, J.W. and Karlson, H.L. (1991). **Theories of Child Abuse and Neglect.** New York: Praeger.

Waterhouse, L. (Ed) (1993). **Child Abuse and Child Abusers.** London: Jessica Kingsley.

West, D.J. and Farrington, D.P. (1977). **The Delinquent Way of Life.** London: Heinemann Educational.

Wilson, H. (1980). Parental Supervision: A neglected aspect of delinquency. *British Journal of Criminology, 20(3),* 203-235.

Wodarski, J.S., Kurtz, P.D., Gaudin, J.M. and Howing, P.T. (1990). Maltreatment and the school-aged child: major academic, socio-emotional and adaptive outcomes. *Social Work, (35)6,* 506-513.

Wolock, I. and Horowitz, B. (1984). Child maltreatment as a social problem: the neglect of neglect. *American Journal of Orthopsychiatry, (54)4,* 530-543.

Wright, C. M. (1992). The Parkin Project – First Report. Unpublished Report.

Wright, C. M. (1996). Research on Failure to Thrive in Newcastle. Unpublished Lecture. Newcastle University.

Appendices

CHILD NEGLECT WORKSHOP

Agency...............................

Gender...............................

Individual Exercise One: Definition

Define child neglect in your own words. Try to make your definition simple and concise.
(This is not an essay question!)

CHILD NEGLECT WORKSHOP - CASE SCENARIOS

Agency...

Gender...

Case Scenarios	Would you refer?		Standard of Child Care					
			dangerously neglectful				adequate (non-neglectful)	
	Yes	No	0	1	2	3	4	5
1. A 10 year old girl is home alone from 3.30pm to 6.30pm Mondays to Fridays.								
2. A parent with a drink problem allows their 12 year old child to drink form their beer mug								
3. A child consistently wears clothing that is ill-fitting and in a poor state of repair								
4. A primary school age child is expected to prepare his own meals almost daily								
5. A ten year old goes to school tired every day. She admits to having no set bedtime and sleeps on the living room couch								
6. A child often witnesses his mother being physically abused by his father								
7. A parent has not taken care of necessary repairs around the house, there is broken glass on the front doorstep								
8. Parents with learning difficulties are unable to rid their infant of nappy rash. The GP is concerned about the baby's health								
9. A child is often seen outside on a cold winter's day with no hat, mittens, and only a light jacket								
10. A 13 year old child does not go to school and the parents do not attempt to intervene								
11. There are no carpets at all in the house								
12. An 8 year old child is left at night to baby-sit three younger siblings while the parent works.								
13. A parent was to pick up his/her child from the baby-sitter at 4.00pm and did not return until the next day. This was the second time this has happened.								
14. A young mother of 3 children often uses her benefit on non-food items such as beer and cigarettes								
15. A parent leaves an infant in an unlocked car for 15 minutes whilst she is in the supermarket								
16. A 5 year old consistently smells of urine. She is isolated at school and her classmates bully her								
17. A child is often ignored when he tries to tell his parent something and is pushed aside when he shows a need for love								
18. A nurse who is a single parent has two children (aged 11 and 2). Her shifts mean sometimes leaving the children on their own for a few hours some days. There have never been any problems								
19. A child does not have appropriate toys and the parents make no effort to obtain them								
20. A parent seems not to follow through on threatened punishments and very frequently no action is taken when discipline is required								
21. A child suffers from an ongoing illness and is not receiving essential medical care								
22. A parent frequently screams obscenities at the child and the child cries								
23. A family relies on state benefit and does not spend money wisely, often running out of food by the end of the week								
24. A 12 year old child has never been to the dentist								
25. Three children in a family are in special education classes and regularly miss one or two days of school a week								
26. A 12 year old child is required to do all the housework								
27. A child begs for food. The child has not eaten in a day								
28. A primary school age child eats lunch at school but has no hot meals at home								
29. A child does not have a bath for a week at a time								
30. A 9 year old child is required to provide the discipline for her younger siblings								

CHILD NEGLECT CASES - SURVEY

Subject

          name: code

          age (at registration)

          gender

          ethnicity

          siblings (ordinal position)

          family structure

          legal status

Keyworker

          name: code

          gender

          ethnicity

          years qualified

          generic/specialist

          child protection training

          neglect training

Keyworker Interview

These structured questions relate to the situation as at registration. The following factors have been identified by groups of practitioners as significant features of neglect cases. In the sample case we are considering are the following significant features in this case? Answer: yes, no, don't know.

a) **Child**

delayed development
lack of stimulation
behaviour problems
aggression
physical injury/abuse
sexual abuse/disinhibited sexuality
frozen awareness
poor hygiene
hunger/feeding problems/inadequate diet
failure to thrive
health problems/inappropriate medical requests

b) **Parents/Caregivers**

poor parenting of caregivers
history of neglect/abuse in caregivers
caregivers experienced care system/prison
substance abuse
mental illness/learning disability
inability to nurture/lack of bonding
poor parenting skills
disorganisation/mismanagement

c) **Family Dynamics**

high stress levels
family violence
unrealistic expectations of child
parents needs first
scapegoating
lack of boundaries

d) **Supervision**

lack of supervision
inappropriate carers

e) **Compliance**

family known to SSD (before this episode)
resistant/non-cooperative
fail to keep appointments
poor school attendance

f) **Social Factors**

poverty/deprivation
debts, financial problems
unemployment, reliance on benefits
poor housing
social isolation

Keyworker Interview: free questions

Recognition
Are there any other important factors not mentioned already?
What was the source of the referral?
What, in your opinion, is the most worrying aspect of the case?

Causation
What do you think caused this child to become neglected?
Where do you think intervention should be concentrated in this case – on physical and material conditions, on emotional/relationship issues, or on both together?

Working together
Were significant differences of opinion expressed about registration?
Is there a functioning core group with a clear child protection plan?
Do you feel supported by colleagues from other agencies in your work with this family?

Feelings
Are you optimistic for the future of this child?
Do you feel that you personally have made a difference, for the better, in the life of this child?
How frequently do you receive supervision in this case, and does supervision address the feelings provoked by working this case?

Conclusion
How can the ACPC improve its services to neglecting families?